Madam Butterfly

MASTERWORKS OF OPERA

General Editor: Charles Osborne

MOSCO CARNER

Madam Butterfly

A GUIDE TO THE OPERA

FOREWORD BY
VICTORIA
DE LOS ANGELES

BARRIE & JENKINS

Designed and produced by Breslich & Foss, London

© Breslich & Foss 1979

First published in 1979 by Barrie & Jenkins
An imprint of the Hutchinson Publishing Group
3 Fitzroy Square, London W1P 6JD

Design: Craig Dodd
Picture Research: Philippa Lewis

Filmset and printed in Great Britain by
BAS Printers Limited, Over Wallop, Hampshire

ISBN 0 214 20680 7

Contents

Foreword by
Victoria de los Angeles

Singing *Madam Butterfly* has always been a happy experience for me, first because she is such a fascinating and sympathetic character, and secondly because Puccini is so generous with the beautiful music he gives her. It is not easy, however, to interpret her character in a way that is worthy of the composer, who looked so closely into her heart and expressed her feelings so perfectly in his music. She is a sentimental creature, but for me she is also very real.

At the beginning Butterfly must be shown as a completely trusting and artless young girl, which is the most difficult thing for an adult artist to do. She is so naïve, yet she is also so passionate. She grows up into a woman in the course of the love duet, and in the second act, which takes place three years later, she has become a mother with a sense of maturity and pride. She is so honest herself, so completely true to Pinkerton, that she cannot believe he could betray her after he has given her such assurances of his love, and she is certain that their child binds them together for ever. Her goodness gives her dignity, just as, in the last act, it gives her the will to sacrifice her life for the husband and the child she loves so selflessly. She has great strength of character as well as tenderness.

The role is very demanding musically, because Butterfly is on the stage, singing, almost throughout the opera. No other Puccini heroine has such demands made of her, not Mimì, Tosca or Turandot, but no other character is given music of such variety. There is so much inspiration in all her music, not only in the set arias—the Entrance, '*Un bel dì*' and the Death Scene—but in little phrases all the way through the score. There are brief snatches of melody which are memorable because they express Butterfly's thoughts and feelings with such truth. And if the singer is to be true to the character and the music, she must take corresponding care: she must understand Butterfly with the heart as well as the voice, never exaggerating or appearing in any way sophisticated. It is also necessary to nurture the voice carefully in the early scenes, because at the end comes the most taxing aria of all.

I have been fortunate enough to sing Butterfly on the stage and in recordings with some wonderful Pinkertons—Jussi Björling, for instance, who was so stylish, and Giuseppe di Stefano who always sang with such passion and warmth. I have also known some strange 'babies'—one who kept telling me while I was holding him close to me that he wanted to be sick, another who I did not realise until after the performance was a dwarf older than myself! I have also sung in many very different productions, one of which I remember especially because at the end my costume made me look like a real butterfly pinned on a collector's board. But always I have marvelled that Puccini had created for all time a character who is so essentially feminine, a character who presents a challenge to the singer which is so difficult and yet so rewarding.

Madam Butterfly

OPERA IN TWO ACTS BY
GIACOMO PUCCINI

Background to the Opera

Scarcely had the ink on *Tosca* dried (autumn 1899) before Puccini, as usual, began a frantic search for a suitable new subject. Old plans were taken up and dropped again and new ones considered; among the latter the idea of basing an opera on Alphonse Daudet's once-celebrated burlesque novel *Tartarin de Tarragon* held his attention, on and off, for five years. It was the first time that Puccini's thoughts had veered in the direction of a comic work, thoughts not to be realized until eighteen years later in *Gianni Schicchi*. The right subject was to be found not among the 'thousand suggestions' that kept raining down on the composer, but in a play he saw in London in the summer of 1900. He had come to supervize the first English production of *Tosca* at Covent Garden when his attention was drawn to a one-act drama, *Madam Butterfly*, by David Belasco, which was running in a double bill (with Jerome's *Miss Nobbs*) at the Duke of York Theatre, to full houses.

Belasco had drawn his play from a realistic story by the Philadelphia lawyer, John Luther Long, which dealt with the attempted suicide of a little geisha who had been deserted by an American naval officer to whom she had borne a child. This story appeared in the *Century Magazine* in 1898 and was based on a real incident that had taken place in Nagasaki. The historical Butterfly was one Tsuru Yamamura (1851–88), who had a child by a wealthy English merchant, and whose attempt at *hara-kiri*, after his desertion, had been frustrated. Her son was later taken by his father to an American missionary school in Nagasaki. Long had never been to Japan himself, but his sister, who knew the country from long first-hand experience as the wife of an American missionary in Nagasaki, provided him with authentic details about its customs and mores, and told him about the sad episode of the geisha. Belasco, then at the height of his career as a playwright and theatrical producer, was so deeply impressed by the story's suitability for the dramatic stage

LEFT: *David Belasco, American producer and author of many plays, among them the one-act* Madam Butterfly

that in collaboration with Long he adapted it into a one-act play, which was given in New York (with his own farce, *Naughty Anthony*) on 5 March 1900, when it created a sensation.

Seven weeks later, Belasco brought it to London, where it repeated its American success. Puccini, who knew no English and was therefore unable to follow its dialogue, was nevertheless profoundly gripped by it, which fact was excellent proof to him of the remarkable power and effectiveness of Belasco's drama. The heroine and her fate struck a deep chord in him and the exotic setting fascinated him. According to Belasco (who was not always a trustworthy witness), Puccini came into the green room after the performance, embraced the playwright and begged him to grant permission to base an opera on the play. 'I agreed at once', relates Belasco, 'and told him he could do anything he liked with the play and make any sort of contract because it is not possible to discuss business arrangements with an impulsive Italian, who has tears in his eyes and both his arms round your neck.'

The contract was signed in April 1901—nine months after Belasco had agreed to give *Madam Butterfly* to the 'impulsive Italian'—and work on the libretto could now begin in all earnest by Puccini's two trusted and highly experienced collaborators, Giuseppe Giacosa and Luigi Illica, the librettists of *La Bohème* and *Tosca*. In spring 1902, at Illica's suggestion, Puccini met the celebrated Japanese actress Sada Jacco, who happened to be visiting Milan in the course of a rapid tour through Italy and France where she appeared to great acclaim in Japanese plays. The composer wanted to hear her speak in her native tongue so as to obtain a first-hand impression of the timbre and range of a female Japanese voice with its, for European ears, high twitter.

About the same time, he also had meetings with the wife of the Japanese ambassador to Italy, who said that she had known of the real incident with the little geisha, and 'told me many interesting things and sang me some native songs'. On hearing Puccini's outline of the libretto, however, she criticized the choice of names for the different characters, considering them inappropriate, particularly that of Prince Yamadori, which she found to be 'feminine' and therefore unsuitable: the tradition of the Japanese theatre demands that the characters be given names suggestive of their sex. (As the opera shows, Puccini paid no heed to this custom.) Always a perfectionist, he consulted, in addition, gramophone records of Japanese music and books on customs, religious ceremonies and architecture. He almost

became a student of Far Eastern ethnography, as happened again some twenty years later for *Turandot*.

Compared with the labours involved in the fashioning of the libretti for *Manon Lescaut* and *La Bohème*, the operatic adaptation of Belasco's play proceeded fairly smoothly, except for one serious hitch in November 1902 when Puccini suddenly decided to omit the second of the three acts and compress the remaining two into a single act (just like the American drama) but preceded by a Prologue (the present Act I). On 29 November Puccini began the orchestration of the opening act and, with all obstacles cleared, the opera might have been finished considerably earlier than it was (December 1903), had Puccini not been involved in a motor accident on 25 February 1903 on the way from Lucca to his home at Torre del Lago. In addition to a number of contusions, the composer sustained a fracture of the right shin bone, which was set so badly at first that it had to be broken again and reset. This left him with a permanent limp, and for nearly three years he had to walk with a stick. (A wound sustained in the accident, which would not heal, led to the

TOP LEFT: *Giulio Ricordi, Puccini's publisher and his paternal friend and mentor*

TOP RIGHT: *Puccini (left) with his collaborators on* Madam Butterfly, *Giacosa and Illica. Giulio Ricordi, the composer's publisher, called the three the 'Holy Trinity'*

TOP LEFT: *Giovanni Zenatello (Pinkerton) and Giuseppe De Luca (Sharpless) appeared in the disastrous opening performance at La Scala, Milan on 17 February 1904*

TOP RIGHT: *Rosina Storchio, the first Butterfly*

discovery that Puccini was suffering from a mild form of diabetes.) His convalescence took a full eight months, though in the spring he was allowed to leave his bed and repair to the piano (like Schumann, Wagner, Stravinsky and Alban Berg, Puccini was a 'piano composer') by means of a wheel-chair. The first, and in the event only, performance of the original version of *Madam Butterfly* was fixed to take place at La Scala on 17 February 1904. Under the management of Giulio Gatti-Casazza (later manager of the Metropolitan Opera in New York), no effort was spared to mount the opera in style. The stage designs were by the renowned French theatre painter, Lucien Jusseaume, and Tito Ricordi, the son of Puccini's publisher, was the producer. The cast was resplendent: Butterfly was sung by Rosina Storchio, a highly gifted and intelligent young singer recently introduced to La Scala by Toscanini; Pinkerton was Giovanni Zenatello and Sharpless, the American Consul, was the famous Giuseppe de Luca. The performance was conducted by Cleofonte Campanini, who subsequently often appeared during the Italian seasons at Covent Garden.

Puccini had never before been so confident of the success of an opera of his as he was of *Madam Butterfly*, into which he had, in his own words, put all his heart and soul, and which he considered the best and most modern of his works. At the rehearsals the enthusiasm of all the participants, from the singers down to the stage-hands, was tremendous, and at the end of the dress rehearsal the orchestra spontaneously rose to a man to give Puccini an ovation. In previous years he had always been at pains to discourage members of his family from attending the first nights of his operas, not wishing to expose them to the 'uncertainties of a first experiment'. This time he felt so assured of success that he made a special point of inviting his sister Ramelde and her daughter, and he had his eighteen-year-old son Tonio with him in the wings.

Puccini's expectations were dashed in a manner rare in operatic history and even worse than the fiascos at the first productions of *La Traviata* in Venice and *Carmen* in Paris. Here is how Giulio Ricordi (who himself felt—wrongly—that the opera was a 'feather-weight') described the evening in the March 1904 edition of *Musica e Musicisti*:

First performance of *Madam Butterfly*, libretto by Illica and Giacosa, music by Puccini. Growls, shouts, groans, laughter, giggling, the usual single cry of *bis*, designed to excite the public still more; that sums up the reception which the public of La Scala accorded the new work by Maestro Giacomo Puccini. After this pandemonium, throughout which virtually nothing could be heard, the public left the theatre pleased as Punch. Never before had one seen so many happy or joyous faces—satisfied as though all had shared in a general triumph. In the vestibule the joy was at its height and there was no lack of those who rubbed their hands, underlining this gesture with the great words: *consummatum est, parce sepulto*! The spectacle given in the auditorium seemed as well organized as that on the stage, since it began precisely with the beginning of the opera.

This is an accurate account of the evening, after which the authors, Puccini, Giacosa and Illica, in agreement with the publishers, withdrew *Madam Butterfly* and returned to the management of La Scala the fee for the rights of production,

TOP LEFT: *Puccini, who loved motor cars, had an accident which left him with a permanent limp and delayed the completion of* Madam Butterfly

TOP RIGHT: *Caricature of Puccini driving a car with Butterfly standing behind him*

notwithstanding their determination to produce the opera again.

It is worth describing this evening in some detail, if only to become aware of the depths to which an audience influenced by intrigues and cabals is capable of sinking. After some noise at the beginning, the first act, up to the entrance of Butterfly and her friends, was listened to in silence. The first serious disturbance occurred at the point where she sings the expansive phrase '*spira sul mare e sulla terra*': the passage was greeted with angry shouts of 'That is from *Bohème*!' Still, seeing the Italian public's susceptibility to 'reminiscences', there was perhaps nothing exceptional in these shouts. The remainder of the act passed quietly enough but the end of the long love duet was greeted with hisses and catcalls, mingled with applause that brought three curtain calls, two of which were taken by Puccini, who limped on to the stage with a stick. The real fracas was reserved for the second act. There was a harmless incident on the stage when, at a swift movement by Rosina Storchio, her kimono billowed up in front of her, which elicited the ironic comment 'Butterfly is pregnant!' Both her aria '*Un bel dì vedremo*' and her scene with Yamadori were received with apathy. After the 'Letter' scene with Sharpless there was some applause which turned, however, into an uproar of hisses, obscene sneers, sarcastic laughter and demands of *bis*! when Butterfly

16

introduced her child to the Consul. The uproar reached its height at the end of Butterfly's all-night vigil when Tito Ricordi, in trying to outdo Belasco's realism, had arranged for the imitation of a whole 'concert' of twittering birds to mark the break of dawn. The audience, by now in a hilarious mood, capped this piece of silliness with its own brand of bird and animal cries. As one writer put it, La Scala resembled a menagerie more than an opera house that evening. The fate of the opera was sealed. Although its tragic *dénouement* succeeded in damping the high spirits in the auditorium, the curtain descended to the accompaniment of whistling, howls and derisive laughter.

What was Puccini's state of mind after this evening? Writing to a friend the next day, he described it as 'lynching. Those cannibals didn't listen to a single note!' And four days later, to the same friend:

I am still shocked by all that happened—not so much for what they did to my poor Butterfly, but for all the poison they spat on me as an artist and as a man. . . . They have printed all kinds of things! Now they say that I am going to rewrite the opera and that it will take me six months! Nothing of the kind! I am not rewriting anything or, at least, very few

BELOW: *Costume designs for the first performance at La Scala: Butterfly (left), Suzuki (centre), Pinkerton (right)*

RIGHT: *Puccini as Captain of the yacht* Cio-cio-san *bought from the royalties of the opera, with his step-granddaughter Bicchi*

details—I shall make a few cuts and divide the second act into two parts—something which I had already thought of doing during the rehearsals, but it was then too near the first night. . . . That first night was a Dantean Inferno, prepared in advance.

'Prepared in advance', wrote Puccini. Indeed there was more in the fiasco at La Scala than meets the eye. Admittedly, the composer had made some miscalculations. In deciding to cast the opera in two acts only, the first of which lasted nearly an hour and the second an hour and a half, he did not reckon with the limited stamina of the Milan public in those days, when a Wagner opera could not be given without considerable cuts. There were, in addition, a number of scenic and musical details in Act I which collectively rendered the original version of the opera less effective than its revised version; to what extent will be seen in a discussion of the first version. Yet one thing is certain: the differences between the two versions are by no means marked enough to provide the sole explanation for the flood of abuse and ridicule that was poured on the opera at La Scala, while three months later at Brescia, with almost the same public as in Milan, the revised version was received with enthusiastic acclaim. True, documentary evidence for the real cause of the *débâcle* is lacking, and even Ricordi and Puccini confine themselves to vague allegations. Yet it is safe to suggest that the scandal at La Scala on the night of 17 February 1904 had all the appearances of having been engineered and organized by a group of Puccini's rivals and enemies, who were trying to ruin the performance by all means at their disposal. And this meant, in the first place, the hiring of a claque; there are indeed descriptions of the amount of whistling, shouting and barracking that could be bought from the Milanese claque in those days.

The reception by the press of *Madam Butterfly* can be gauged from the sensational headlines that appeared the next morning: *'Puccini Hissed'*, *'Fiasco at La Scala'*, *'Butterfly, Diabetic Opera, Result of an Accident'*. A writer of *Il Secolo*, announcing the cancellation of the second performance of the opera and its replacement by *Faust*, gave it as his considered opinion that:

> A second performance would have provoked a scandal which would have called for decided action on the part of the Milan public, who do not relish being mocked. This opera is not one of those (like *The Barber of Seville*) which carry the seeds of resurrection in them. It reveals that Maestro Puccini was in a hurry. Importuned as he was to bring out the work this season, sick as he was, he did not find original inspiration and had recourse to melodies from his previous operas, and even helped himself to other composers' melodies. In his defence we must say that the libretto was artistically unfortunate. . . . The opera is dead.

Yet what was the judgment of serious and fair-minded critics who tried to preserve a more objective attitude towards Puccini's new opera? It was by no means as negative and

damning as that of the majority of their colleagues. Thus the strictures which Giovanni Pozza of *Il Corriere della Sera* made are fully supported by a critical study of the original version. For instance, he criticized the length and disproportion of the two acts, suggesting 'many and courageous cuts', notably in the first act in which the action loses itself in minute superfluous details and 'where the music is at times unnecessarily repetitive and prolix'. Pozza also faulted Puccini's insistent use of reminiscences, which was 'imprudent, risky and little pleasing'. What is strange, however, is his statement that the 'synthetic form of Puccini's melodies is unable to express the rapid succession of changes in both the situation and the sentiments of the child-like Butterfly', since it is in this very opera that Puccini evinces consummate skill in his command of melodic mosaics woven into a continuous web and reflecting every shade of the heroine's emotional reactions. No doubt, as with *La Bohème*, the fragmentary impressionist style of the opera, coupled with the novelty of its harmonic language, created obstacles for the ears of Puccini's older contemporaries, for whom even Debussy was still a fearful iconoclast. Pozza, however, fully acknowledged Puccini's genius in evoking an exotic atmosphere, and he singled out for special praise the 'Letter' and 'Flower' scenes. He came to the conclusion that, 'while the opera has not stood the test, I yet persist that shortened and made lighter it will rise again'. He was to be proved right three months later.

For Puccini, the fiasco of the original *Madam Butterfly* was a blow he could not forget for many years to come. Yet he was convinced that in it he had written the 'most heartfelt and most expressive opera' he had conceived and that, given in a smaller theatre 'less permeated by hatred and passion', it would rise and conquer. He subjected it to what he called '*piccoli lavorucci*' ('small, insignificant revisions') though, as we shall see, they were not as small as he made them out to be. Since *Madam Butterfly* is essentially an intimate domestic tragedy with a sole protagonist, a smaller theatre was (and in this writer's view is always) preferable to a big house. Turin, Bologna and Genoa were considered until the choice fell on Brescia, near Milan, where the revised version was given on 28 May, with a new and excellent singer, Salomea Krusceniski, in the title role; Pinkerton was again Zenatello, and Sharpless was sung by Virgilio Bellatti. The evening was a triumphant success, fully vindicating the composer's unshaken confidence in his work. '*Butterfly, rinnegata e felice*', as Puccini aptly quoted from the libretto, was launched on her world conquest.

Background to the Libretto

Puccini's little geisha has both an operatic and a literary ancestry. Her operatic lineage, somewhat older, can be traced back to two heroines of French romantic opera: Selica in Meyerbeer's *L'Africaine* (1865) and Lakmé, the protagonist of Delibes's entrancing opera of that name (1883). (The intrinsic situation, though, and the larger theme implied in it, was anticipated as early as 1689 by Purcell's *Dido and Aeneas*.) Like Butterfly, they belong to non-European races; like her, they fall in love with a white man, thus offending against a sacred taboo of their people, and all three commit suicide after their lovers abandon them to return to their native lands. It is the clash between different cultures, the incompatibility of East and West, and by implication the alleged white man's superiority over other races, as seen through the eyes of the nineteenth century. As Butterfly tells Pinkerton in Act I of the original version of Puccini's opera, it was the thought that he was 'an American, a barbarian', that first made her recoil from marriage to him.

These subjects were doubtless based on real incidents that occurred in the second half of the nineteenth century, when countries long considered far-off and legendary were, through expanding commerce and colonization, brought into contact with the West. The Near or Middle East, lying in geographical proximity to Europe, had seen its operatic exploitation in the so-called 'Turkish' operas of the eighteenth century. With the Far East, notably Japan, this happened much later. For it was not until the 1860s, after a self-imposed seclusion lasting for over two centuries, that Japan began to lower its barriers against the West. Foreign navies—French, British, American and Russian—were allowed to call at her ports, and it was a French naval captain and writer, Pierre Loti, who produced what was probably the first novel about the land of cherry-blossom, chrysanthemums, geishas and samurai. Loti's auto-

biographical romance *Madame Chrysanthème* (1887) appears to have set off the fashion for Japanese subjects in western literature and opera. There were the writings of Lafcadio Hearn, Basil Hall and Rutherford Alcock, and there was the spate of musical stage works, such as Sullivan's *The Mikado* (1885), Messager's *Madame Chrysanthème* (based on Loti's novel), *The Geisha* (1896) and *San Toy* (1899) by Jones, Mascagni's *Iris* (1898) and the Puccini opera. The first composer in this field, however, was Saint-Saëns, with his little-known and charming one-act opera, *La Princesse Jaune* (1873).

ABOVE: *A Japanese print showing the arrival of the American Navy under Commodore Perry in 1876*

Loti's novel, which has both a direct and an indirect bearing on Puccini's libretto, takes the form of a diary kept by Pierre (the author), a naval officer on the *Triumphante*, during his ship's anchorage at Nagasaki from July to September 1885. To while away the time, he avails himself of a strange Japanese institution whereby officers of foreign navies could buy and 'marry' a geisha for the length of their shore leave. Knowing that their association will be short-lived, both parties of the 'marriage' enter into it in a spirit of *carpe diem*, of living for the day and making the most of it. There is, hence, no tragedy when after three months Pierre rejoins his ship, and any feeling of remorse or guilt he might have entertained for abandoning his 'wife' is completely dispelled when, bidding her farewell, he finds the geisha counting the coins he gave her as a parting present and testing them with a hammer, 'with the competence and dexterity of an old money-lender'. On the face of it, Loti's geisha would seem to have little in common with Puccini's heroine, but it is in Pierre's description of her during their love idyll that we recognize features characteristic of Butterfly. Chrysanthème is child-like, affectionate, tender and playful—'a little creature made to laugh, yet easily saddened'. Loti's poetic touches are seen not only in his entrancing portrait of the refined geisha, but also in his description of the atmosphere that surrounds her and in the delicacy with which he presents her fragile world of tiny, quaint things, all of which come to life in Act I of Puccini's opera. The novel has no proper plot; it excels in the evocation of exquisite moods and impressions, and there is much in it to remind us of Mürger's *Scènes de la vie de Bohème*, even as Puccini's musical characterization of Butterfly reminds us of that of Mimì.

Long, the author of the story in the *Century Magazine*, took over elements from the Loti novel, but it was he who, following the authentic incident at Nagasaki, introduced a semi-tragic twist: Butterfly, after a visit to the American Consulate, where she meets Kate Pinkerton and guesses that Kate is Pinkerton's wife and that he will never come back to her, tries to commit *hara-kiri*; she has already wounded herself when the thought of the child she has had by Pinkerton makes her change her mind. When, at the end of Long's story, Kate arrives at the geisha's house to take the child with her, she finds it deserted, the implication being that Butterfly has returned to her former profession—the alternative that Puccini's heroine rejects in her second-act aria, *'Che tua madre'*. Long's tale is too drawn-out for its simple plot, and was a rather crude sketch showing a 'slice of life' of Japan at the turn of the nineteenth century. And, while Loti's Chrysanthème was a refined, gentle and delightfully amusing girl, the geisha of the American story is a silly, love-sick creature, insisting that 'no one shall speak anythin' but those United States languages in these Lef-ten-ant Pik-ker-ton's house', and assuring all and sundry that her marriage to the American naval officer 'make me mos' bes' happy female

woman in Japan—mebby in that whole worl', w'at you thing?' (This sentence is, largely, retained in Puccini's libretto but in transmogrified form: '*Io sono la fanciulla la più lieta del Giappone, anzi del mondo.*') The name of Loti's geisha is Ki-Hou-San, supposed to mean Chrysanthemum, which Long changed to Cho-Cho-San and anglicized into Butterfly, possibly from the butterfly crest worn at the back of their dress by all geishas: in the opera, Pinkerton, in his dialogue with the American Consul (Act I), compares his bride to this delicate insect.

Loti's French captain Pierre, a charmingly frivolous and witty character of polished manners, is metamorphosed by Long into the callous and fatuous Benjamin Franklin Pinkerton of the American Navy, who is a practical joker and fancies himself as a modern Pygmalion. As Sharpless reflects, it was 'exactly in Pinkerton's line to take this dainty, vivid, eager and formless material [Butterfly] and mould it to his most wantonly whimsical wish', adding drily that it was 'perhaps fortunate for Butterfly that his country had need of him so soon after his marriage'. Also Pierre regards his bride as 'a quaint toy' ('*un jouet bizarre*') and feels himself to be her lord and master, yet he

ABOVE: *The character of Butterfly was based on a real geisha who was deserted by a wealthy English merchant*

never makes a wounding remark about her and her people, whereas the Pinkerton of Long, Belasco and, partly, Puccini, becomes positively offensive in his condescension and feeling of superiority as an American.

Of the characters in Long that are directly modelled on those in the French novel there is, first, Kan-Goo-Rou, 'a rare combination of interpreter, laundryman and discreet agent for the crossing of races', who is turned into Goro, the grotesque marriage broker; while Chrysanthème's young friend Oyouki becomes Butterfly's devoted servant Suzuki. Long added three more characters who may have figured in the historical incident or were of his own invention. The first of these is the American Consul, Sharpless, who is a little grave and pompous, a little boring and colourless, honest, good-hearted and gentle—more or less the figure we meet in the Puccini opera. There is, secondly, Prince Yamadori, described by Long as 'one of those modern pensioned princes in Japan, a matrimonial article and preternaturally fascinating'. And, finally, there is Kate Pinkerton, who is a shadowy figure in Belasco's play and in the opera but plays a more important role in Long's story.

The sensation that the story created on its publication is to be explained by the fact that, for its time, the subject was a most unusual one, that in his treatment of it Long succeeded in rendering the characters credible in their particular setting, and that he introduced situations of an unfailingly moving nature, such as Butterfly's visit to the American Consulate and her accidental meeting there with an unknown blonde woman (Kate), whose identity she does not take long to guess. Perhaps the most poignant situation, and one that is certainly unique, is Butterfly's vigil for Pinkerton's return, which Long describes as follows:

Not for a night, but for days and nights, eating little, sleeping little—less and less of these. Finally, Cho-Cho-San could no longer hold the glass with which she was scanning the harbour for Pinkerton's ship. She lay on the mats with the baby, while the youthful handmaid watched. Every day the faded flowers were replaced by purchased ones—cheaper and cheaper ones. And there one day by accident Cho-Cho-San sees Pinkerton on deck with a blonde woman on his arm, and on the following morning the warship had disappeared.

Duke of York's Theatre.
ST. MARTIN'S LANE, W.C.

Sole Lessee and Manager ... ... Mr. CHARLES FROHMAN

EVERY EVENING at 8 O'CLOCK,
Mr. CHARLES FROHMAN'S
Duke of York's Theatre Company
Present a Comedy, in Four Acts, entitled

MISS HOBBS

By JEROME K. JEROME.

Woolf Kingsearl	... ...	Mr. HERBERT WARING
Percival Kingsearl	... ...	Mr. ALLAN AYNESWORTH
George Jessop	... ...	Mr. COSMO STUART
Captain Sands	... ...	Mr. J. W. MACDONALD
Charles ...	... (a Page)	Mr. GEORGE CURTISS
Mrs. Kingsearl	... ...	Miss AGNES MILLER
Miss Susan Abbey	... ...	Miss SUSIE VAUGHAN
Millicent Farey	... ...	Miss IDA YEOLAND
Jane	... ...	Miss GENEVRA CAMPBELL
Miss Hobbs ...	... ...	Miss EVELYN MILLARD

Act I. Drawing-Room at Percival Kingsearl's House, Cowes, I.W. Act II. The Mill House, near Cowes
Act III....Cabin of the Yacht "Good Chance." Act IV. ... Same as Act I.
TIME ... ... SUMMER SEASON AT COWES.

At 10 o'clock,

MADAME BUTTERFLY

By DAVID BELASCO, from John Luther Long's Japanese Story.

Cho-Cho-San ...	... (Madame Butterfly)	Miss EVELYN MILLARD
Mr. Sharpless ...	(American Consul)	Mr. CLAUDE GILLINGWATER
Lieut. B. F. Pinkerton	(of the Warship Connecticut)	Mr. ALLAN AYNESWORTH
Yamadori ...	... (a Citizen of New York) ...	Mr. WILLIAM H. DAY
Nakado	(a Marriage Broker)	Mr. J. C. BUCKSTONE
Suzuki ...	... (a Maid)	Miss SUZIE VAUGHAN
Kate ...	... ...	Miss JANET EVELYN SOTHERN

Scene—The little house at the foot of Higashi Hill facing the seaport harbour.
Incidental Music by WILLIAM FURST from the Empire Theatre, New York. Scenery by ERNEST GROS, from Empire Theatre, New York.
Note—At one period of this play a night passes, and the action is taken up on the following morning
The production under the personal direction of DAVID BELASCO.

OVERTURE	..."Le Brasseur de Preston" ... Adam	FANTASIE	... ...	"Carmen"...	... Bizet
DANCES	...." Bourée et Gigue" ... German	GRAND MARCH	...	"Tannhauser"	... Wagner
SELECTION	... "The Rose of Persia" ... Sullivan				

Matinee every Saturday at 2 o'clock.

Mr. Charles Frohman announces that the next season of THE DUKE OF YORK'S THEATRE
COMPANY will begin in September, presenting a New Play by HENRY ARTHUR JONES.

General Manager for Mr Charles Frohman ... ... Mr. W. LESTOCQ

GARRICK THEATRE.—Every Evening, CHARLES FROHMAN'S SEASON, presenting Mrs. LESLIE CARTER
in "ZAZA," David Belasco's Version of Pierre Berton and Charles Simon's Play.
Doors open at 7.30. Commence at 8. Matinees Every Saturday at 2.

Musical Director	... Mr. EDWARD JONES	Stage Manager	...	Mr. FRANCIS NEILSON
Business Manager			...	Mr. JAMES W. MATHEWS

ICES TEA AND COFFEE can be had o the Attendants

G. HARMSWORTH & Co. Printers, 42, Floral Street, Covent Garden 10/5/1900

This, then, was the story which Belasco, with his keen eye for an effective melodrama, adapted into a one-act play. It was Puccini's view that the play was far superior to the story, which, incidentally, Giacosa published in an Italian translation in a noted literary periodical, *Lettura*, in February 1904, to coincide with the first-night of the opera. As a literary figure Belasco was negligible; he had no contact with the intellectual trends of his age and no ideas of his own to advance. His real merit lay in his *mise-en-scène*, which for its time was staggering indeed. His special line as a producer was the creation of romantic illusions by a cunning manipulation of the lighting and of painted curtains which resulted in almost cinematic effects. This was all done to saturate the spectator in the atmosphere of a play before it began. Thus, the opening of *Madam Butterfly* was preceded by

ABOVE: *Playbill of the Duke of York's Theatre where Belasco's* Madam Butterfly *had its London production in late Spring 1900*

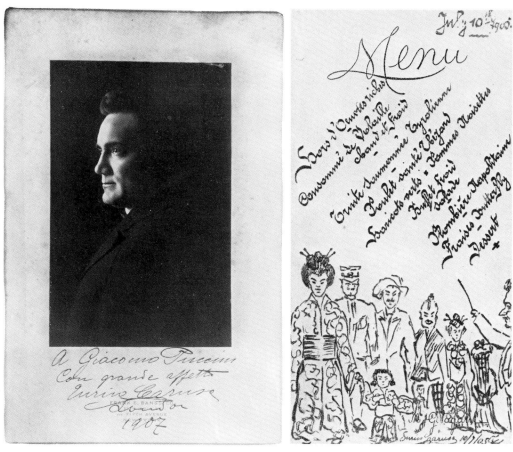

TOP LEFT: *Enrico Caruso who sang Pinkerton in the first London production at Covent Garden in July 1905*

TOP RIGHT: *Caruso's caricature drawn on a menu card of the* Butterfly *cast for the first London production*

a succession of illuminated screens depicting in turn a ricefield, a garden of blossoming cherry trees and a snow-capped volcano in a sunset. It was no doubt an attempt to wed the novel technique of the cinema, then in its infancy, to the theatre. Belasco's greatest *coup*—the one that earned him the epithet 'wizard of the stage'—came in the scene of Butterfly's night vigil. Taking his cue from Long's description of her futile waiting for Pinkerton (see above), he marked the passage of time (twelve hours) by counterfeiting it with a series of changing lighting effects on the open stage: dusk, the gradual appearance of the stars, the break of day accompanied by the chirping of birds, and finally sunrise: this silent scene played for 14 minutes. Belasco himself declared, a few years before his death in 1931, that he had conceived this scene as a challenge to himself, and considered it 'my most successful effort in appealing to the imagination of those who have sat before my stage'.

In dramatizing Long's plot, Belasco made the ending wholly tragic through Butterfly's suicide, and to heighten the pathos of this scene he brought in Pinkerton, who in the story never set eyes on her again after joining his ship. By a skilful elimination and compression of Long's various episodes, he achieved the classical unities of time, place and action, the drama evolving within twenty-four hours in Butterfly's house on the hill overlooking Nagasaki, and beginning with what is Puccini's Act II, Part 1. Belasco, however, retained a great deal of Long's own dialogue and, instead of toning down its crudities and trivial realistic touches, added some of his own, the most notorious being Butterfly's dying words to Pinkerton: 'Too bad those robins did'n' nes' again.' Famous last words indeed.

Puccini's original intention seems to have been to follow Belasco's design and write a one-act opera, but by November 1900 he had thought of two acts, the first to play in America as a kind of Prologue and the second in Japan, suggesting to Illica that he draw for this on Long's magazine story. (The official title of the opera explicitly states 'after John L Long and David Belasco'.) In March 1901 this plan was discarded in favour of a full-length work, which was to consist of a Prologue (the present Act I) and three acts that were to play in *Butterfly's House—The American Consulate—Butterfly's House*. This was Illica's idea because he wanted, for the sake of contrast, to introduce a marked western element into the otherwise wholly Japanese *ambiance* of the opera. For the act in the American Consulate, Illica went back to the episode in Long where Butterfly tries to see the Consul in order to ascertain when Pinkerton's ship will return to Nagasaki. During this visit she meets Kate Pinkerton, with consequences as described above. All was well and Puccini was working full steam ahead when, in mid-November 1902, he was suddenly struck by the idea that the Consulate act was completely superfluous. As he wrote to Ricordi: 'This act was a grave error. The drama must move to its close without interruption, rapid, effective and terrible.' The Consulate act was thrown out and the two remaining acts were compressed into one (Act II), while the Prologue became Act I. Both Giacosa and Illica at first tried their best to dissuade him from what they considered a disproportionate design, and one

29

that therefore carried great risk with the public, but Puccini stuck to his guns and insisted on a long second act, with Butterfly's night vigil playing on the open stage, accompanied by a Humming Chorus offstage, followed by a symphonic Intermezzo. This was one of the features that came in for a good deal of criticism at the Scala performance, and, although (we recall) Puccini thought of dividing the act into two parts during the rehearsals, it was for the Brescia production that this was done. More will be said about it in a later chapter.

As for Act I, Giacosa claimed that it was he and Illica who had the 'sound idea of adding a first act, extraneous to the action'. This is not quite true, for the material for it was derived from allusions in both Long and Belasco to the marriage of Butterfly with Pinkerton. This introductory act, as it may be called, served several purposes, the most important of which, from a dramatic point of view, was to show the heroine in her short-lived happiness so as to make her tragedy all the more poignant. This in turn necessitated rendering Pinkerton a far more important character than he is in both the story and the play; indeed, in the latter he does not appear until the very end. This may well have been at the composer's urging, for what Puccini opera could do without a love duet for tenor and soprano? And in *Madam Butterfly* it occupies over fifty pages in slow tempo! Furthermore, this expository act afforded the composer the opportunity for a leisurely setting of the exotic atmosphere, both scenically and musically, and we know that atmosphere-painting was a potent stimulus in his creative processes. Certain details were derived from Loti's novel and Messager's opera *Madame Chrysanthème*. For instance, Butterfly's uncle, the drunkard Yakusidé (who in the original version of the opera has a scene to himself) is modelled on Loti's 'bonzes', whom Pierre visits one day in their monastery to find that these 'fat, chubby and shorn priests are all-too-fond of our French liqueurs—Benedictine or Chartreuse'. To Puccini's priest it is whisky that appeals most. Episodes taken from the Messager opera include the lovers' meeting for the wedding ceremony, the ceremony itself and the closing love duet; and Puccini was also indebted to Delibes's *Lakmé* for Butterfly's offstage introduction and the 'Flower' duet of Act II. Finally, the motif of the curse uttered by another of the geisha's bonze uncles was evidently found in a hint in Long, in which she is ostracized by her entire family, after adopting her husband's religion.

If we stand back from the dramaturgy of the libretto to cast an overall glance at it, several features will emerge. First, the drama is a tragedy in the classical sense, for the catastrophe is the inevitable outcome of the heroine's *moral* character. Because the geisha is what she is, she cannot act otherwise than she does. Confronted with three alternatives after Sharpless has told her the truth—marriage to the wealthy Prince Yamadori, resumption of her former profession as a dancing girl or death—she chooses death of her own free will. Secondly, Butterfly is the only one among Puccini's heroines to show a continuous, consistent development: from the child-bride of Act I to the tragic woman, the martyr of love, at the end of Act II. Thirdly, the intrinsic action is an inner, psychological one, unfolding inside the geisha, who is the centre of the drama. She has no real antagonist: Pinkerton is no more than a catalyst who sets the tragedy in motion, and Suzuki and Sharpless are, for all the attention they receive from the composer, dramatically speaking mere satellites revolving round Butterfly's planet. Finally, because the little geisha and her fate struck deep into Puccini's imagination—'*grande dolore in piccole anime*' ('great sorrows in little souls')—he was able to probe into her psyche more thoroughly than he did with his other heroines, bringing the totality of his resources to bear on a musico-dramatic illumination of her innermost feelings and thoughts. Thus, *Madam Butterfly* is the only one of his operas to which the term 'psychological music-drama' can, despite the melodramatic nature of the plot, be applied without reservation.

Synopsis of the Plot

ACT I: The scene is laid in a Japanese house and terrace on the hill overlooking the harbour of Nagasaki. The action takes place in the early 1900s.

It is shortly before the wedding of Benjamin Franklin Pinkerton (tenor), Lieutenant of the United States Navy, and Cio-Cio-San, known as Butterfly (soprano). After the rise of the curtain, we see Goro (tenor), a marriage broker and general factotum, showing the bridegroom over the house in which he will live with Butterfly. With many obsequious genuflections, Goro explains the strange but extremely practical arrangements of the house in which by means of sliding doors the aspect of the rooms can be changed according to the occupant's desire—at the touch of a finger on the partition, the inside can become the outside and vice versa, and the view on the terrace opened and closed. Pinkerton is greatly pleased with the convenience of all this. To show him other amenities of the house, Goro claps his hands to call the three servants, among them Suzuki (mezzo-soprano), who is Butterfly's personal maid. Suzuki makes apposite remarks, reminding Pinkerton of the value of a smile in all human relationships, but as soon as Goro notices that the Lieutenant is getting bored with her flowery language he claps his hands once more and the servants run off into the house.

Goro now enumerates to Pinkerton the guests to be expected at the wedding: the Imperial Commissioner and the Marriage Registrar, the American Consul, Butterfly, her widowed mother and grandmother, her cousins and other blood relations—'a round two dozen'. So much for the ascendants; as for the descendants, Goro says with a malicious smirk, *that* he leaves to 'Your Excellency and the Beautiful Butterfly'. The voice of the Consul (baritone) is heard and he soon appears over the top of the hill, out of breath and gasping for air after his climb. Pinkerton sends Goro away to fetch refreshments and expounds to Sharpless his hedonistic philosophy (aria:

'*Dovunque al mondo*'). The '*Yankee vagabondo*', wandering over the globe on business or pleasure, casts his anchor where and when it suits him, and when he runs into a squall—as now—he consoles himself with the pleasures and loves of the country in which he happens to find himself. He is marrying in 'Japanese' fashion for 999 years, but with a monthly escape clause. The Consul interrupts him several times with a friendly warning about his 'easy-going gospel', and finally, as in duty bound, joins Pinkerton in a toast to 'America forever' (these words are sung in English). Sharpless asks him whether his bride is beautiful. He is answered by Goro, who has overheard the conversation—'Yes, like a garland of fresh flowers, and all for nothing, a mere 100 yen.' He offers to oblige the Consul in the same fashion, which the latter laughingly declines. Turning to Pinkerton, Sharpless asks him what mad desire drove him to this marriage, whereupon the Lieutenant rhapsodizes on the

ABOVE: *José Carreras (Pinkerton), Delme Bryn-Jones (Sharpless), and Francis Egerton (Goro) in a 1975 Covent Garden production*

33

fragile butterfly beauty and charm of his bride (arietta: '*Amore o grillo*'). The Consul now tells him that Butterfly came to the Consulate a few days ago and, though he did not see her, he was struck by the sincerity of expression in her voice—it would be a great pity, he says, to break the delicate wings of this butterfly and, with them, a trusting heart. But Pinkerton brushes this aside with another toast to a 'true American bride!'

At this moment the voices of Butterfly and her girl companions are heard offstage, and they debouch on to the scene with one of the great tunes of the opera (chorus: '*Spira sul mare e sulla terra*'). Commonplaces are exchanged. Sharpless engages Butterfly in conversation in which he learns something about her family and herself—that her people, once wealthy, lost their fortune and that she had to earn her living as a dancing girl. And her father? 'Dead,' she replies, at which her friends fan themselves nervously and in great embarrassment. The Consul

ABOVE: *An English National Opera production at the London Coliseum in March 1977 with Tom Swift (Pinkerton), Nigi Sato (Butterfly) and Della Jones (Suzuki)*

OPPOSITE: *Arrival of Butterfly and her companions at the house on the hill overlooking Nagasaki*

35

then asks her her age. 'Fifteen. I am already too old,' she coyly replies. As the relatives arrive and stare curiously at the two Americans, Pinkerton makes derisory remarks to Sharpless about his future in-laws, acquired, like his bride and the house, on monthly terms. An animated *ensemble* develops, with the women, jealous of Butterfly, voicing unfavourable comments on the bridegroom, and it is only her mother who approves of him. At a sign from Butterfly, all bow before Sharpless and the condescending Pinkerton, to whom Butterfly now proceeds to show her possessions tucked away in the wide sleeves of her kimono—a pipe, a girdle, a fan and so on. She finally pulls out a sheath which, she gravely declares, is sacred to her and cannot be shown in public. While she takes it into the house, Goro explains to Pinkerton that the dagger enclosed in the sheath was the weapon the Mikado sent to her father with the command to commit *hara-kiri*. Butterfly returns and takes out of her sleeve the *ottoké*, small figures representing the souls of her ancestors. She goes on to tell Pinkerton that she had gone yesterday to the mission house to abjure her own religion and adopt the faith of her bridegroom, adding that none of her relatives knows of it. The wedding ceremony now begins, with the Imperial Commissioner reading out the marriage contract, which the pair sign. All the women bow and congratulate the bride— 'Madam Butterfly'—but she, with a raised finger, corrects them—'Madam F. B. Pinkerton'. The two officials and Sharpless depart, the latter not without another word of warning to Pinkerton to be careful with Butterfly. The relatives raise a toast to the pair (chorus: '*O Kami! O Kami!*'), when a furious voice is heard offstage. It is the Uncle Bonze, who has come to utter a fearful curse on Butterfly for having renounced her religion and her people. The relatives join in the malediction, and Pinkerton, with a curt command, drives them all away and they hurry down the hill, still cursing the weeping Butterfly.

Left alone, Pinkerton comforts her and the basic mood is set for the long love duet ('*Viene la sera*'). Suzuki puts Butterfly's night robe on her, and at Pinkerton's sign she and the other two servants withdraw. While night falls and the stars are beginning to appear in the sky, Pinkerton and Butterfly exchange words of rapture and ecstasy, and finally enter the house.

ACT II: The Inside of Butterfly's House. Three years have

LEFT: *Butterfly (Yasuko Hayashi) presents her child to Sharpless (Delme Bryn-Jones) in a 1975 Covent Garden production*

gone by since Pinkerton sailed away without ever communicating with Butterfly. Yet her love for him is unshakable and her faith in his return unwavering.

At the rise of the curtain, the scene shows a room in semi-darkness. Suzuki is crouching before an image of the Buddha and praying for Butterfly. She is convinced that Pinkerton will never set eyes on her again. Butterfly chides her for her belief in the powers of the Japanese gods—the God of the Americans, she says, would be far more responsive if only He were aware of her plight. She asks how much of the money that Pinkerton provided for her before being recalled to America is left. If he does not return soon, replies Suzuki, they will be penniless. But he will come back, says Butterfly, enraged at her maid's remark that no foreign husband has ever returned to his nest. Had he not, she continues, assured her on the day he left that he would come back when 'the little robins build their nest'? She cannot understand why Suzuki is weeping and, full of hope and with a smile, she imagines his home-coming: how a thread of smoke

37

ABOVE: *Butterfly sights Pinkerton's ship. Elisabeth Schwarzkopf (Butterfly) and Monica Sinclair (Suzuki) in Act II (Covent Garden, 1949–50)*

will rise on the horizon and a white ship make for the harbour; how a speck will appear on the hill—it will be he; and how on reaching the top he will call 'Butterfly!'; but she will at first not answer—half in play, half so that she will not die of happiness. Suzuki must banish her fears, for Pinkerton will come back, she knows it (aria: '*Un bel dì vedremo*').

Sharpless is announced. The Consul has not seen Butterfly since her wedding day and she receives him with a burst of joy. He has come with a letter from Pinkerton that he wishes to read to her, but all his attempts to do so are frustrated by her excited interruptions at hearing Pinkerton's name and her irrelevant comments. She would like to ask him a question: on his last day with her, Pinkerton said that he would return when the robins built their nest; in Japan, she says, the robins have already nested 'three times', but perhaps over there they might do so less often. Utterly puzzled, the Consul replies that he has never studied 'ornithology', a word she does not understand. She goes on to tell Sharpless that soon after Pinkerton's departure Goro had tried to introduce her to a number of suitors on the grounds that she is poor and cast off by her family, the latest of these suitors being the wealthy nincompoop Yamadori. At this moment Yamadori, with a train of servants, makes his pompous entry.

Butterfly teases the Prince mercilessly for his passion for her and turns down his marriage proposal. She is already married, she says proudly. But not, Goro interrupts, under Japanese law, according to which a wife deserted is *ipso facto* a wife divorced. Not in America, retorts Butterfly—there things are done differently and she *is* an American woman. While tea is served, and her attention is momentarily distracted, Goro whispers to the Prince and the Consul that Pinkerton's ship has already been signalled. That is, the Consul says, precisely the reason why he has come: to prepare Butterfly for the bitter news that Pinkerton has married an American woman and will never come back to her. After Yamadori and Goro have left, Sharpless again tries to read her Pinkerton's letter, but, consistently thwarted, he grows impatient and asks her point-blank: what would she do if Pinkerton were never to return? After a terrible silence, Butterfly gravely replies: there are only two things she could do—'go back and entertain the people with my songs or else, better, die'. The Consul, deeply moved, counsels her to accept the hand of the wealthy Yamadori, whereupon Butterfly draws herself up rigidly and calls for Suzuki to show the Consul the way out. No sooner has she given the order than, regretting her abruptness to him, she says that her thoughts of death have passed 'as the clouds pass over the ocean'. And, suddenly struck by an idea, she rushes into the other room, fetches the child she has had by Pinkerton and triumphantly shows it to the Consul. Would not his father hasten back, she says, if he knew he had such a beautiful son? Turning to the child, she repeats to him her previous decision— rather die than become a geisha again (aria: 'Che tua madre'). Sharpless, conquering his emotion, kisses the child and asks him his name; Butterfly replies for him: 'My name is now Trouble, but tell my father that on his return it will be Joy.' Profoundly saddened at the thought that a tragedy will now be inevitable, Sharpless leaves. Furious shouts are heard offstage. It is Suzuki, who drags Goro into the room, accusing him of spreading vile rumours in town that nobody knows who the child's father is. Blind with rage, Butterfly runs to the shrine and seizes her father's dagger with which she threatens to kill Goro;

39

but she relents when Suzuki intervenes and takes the child away.

A cannon shot is heard from the harbour, announcing the arrival of a man-o'-war. With the help of a telescope, Butterfly reads the name of Pinkerton's ship, the *Abraham Lincoln*. All were wrong, she triumphantly exclaims: Pinkerton *has* come back to her—she had always been sure he would. She orders Suzuki to gather flowers in the garden and the two women now deck out the room in preparation for Pinkerton's home-coming (duet: '*Scuoti quella fronda*'). As the sun is setting, Butterfly begins to adorn herself and tells Suzuki to bring the child from the other room. She sadly studies her face in the mirror—too many sighs, she reflects, have passed her lips, and too long have her eyes stared into the distance. She takes some carmine to paint her face and puts a dab of colour also on the child's cheeks, lest the vigil before him make him paler than he is. And smilingly she wonders what people are going to say—Uncle Bonze and Yamadori, 'for all of their sneers and contempt'. Butterfly dons her bridal robe and asks Suzuki to put a scarlet poppy in her hair. At her bidding, the maid draws the *shosi* (the sliding shutters) at the back of the room and Butterfly now proceeds to bore three holes in it—one high up for herself, one lower down for Suzuki and a third still lower down for the child, whom she places on a cushion. She stands motionless and rigid like a statue, looking through the highest hole; Suzuki crouches down and looks through her hole; while the child, between them, gazes 'curiously' into the distance. Voices are heard offstage humming a wordless melody. First the child and then Suzuki fall asleep; only Butterfly remains awake, staring out into the night.

An orchestral Intermezzo leads to the next scene. Dawn has come and Butterfly is still standing against the *shosi* and gazing through the hole. Suzuki awakens and urges her mistress to retire with the child into another room and rest from her night-long vigil. She will call her as soon as Pinkerton arrives. Sadly she murmurs, '*Povera Butterfly!*' No sooner has Butterfly left the room than a repeated knock is heard at the door. Opening it, Suzuki utters a cry of immense surprise as she sees Sharpless and Pinkerton standing on the threshold. They motion her to remain quiet and not wake Butterfly. The maid tells them that Butterfly has waited the whole night for Pinkerton and, to his question of how she knew that he had come back, she says that for the past three years the geisha has watched the flag and colour of each ship that crossed the harbour, in expectation of his return. Suzuki suddenly sees a lady in the garden and asks them who she is. Pinkerton has not the courage to tell her the truth, and simply says that that lady came with him. 'She is his wife,' the Consul declares bluntly. Horrified, Suzuki exclaims, 'Hallowed souls of our forefathers, that will be the end of Butterfly!' Sharpless now explains that they have come so early in the morning in the hope of finding Suzuki alone and to enlist her help in their delicate task. The child's future must be protected from trouble and given into the care of Pinkerton's American wife (trio: '*So che alle sue pene*'). Pinkerton, overcome by poignant memories and seized by bitter remorse, decides to

leave without seeing Butterfly (arietta: '*Addio fiorito asil*'). Suzuki goes into the garden to speak to Kate and, moved by her sincerity, promises to convey to her mistress Kate's offer to adopt the child as her own, adding, however, that she must be alone with Butterfly when the mortal blow falls. At that moment Butterfly is heard calling 'Suzuki! Suzuki!' and she rushes into the room, certain to find Pinkerton there. As she does not see him, she excitedly searches in every corner and behind the screen. Noticing Kate and receiving no answer from Suzuki to her question where Pinkerton is, she suspects the truth, but is afraid of understanding it. She asks the maid to tell her whether he is alive—'Yes or no?' 'Yes,' says Suzuki. Butterfly stands transfixed. 'But he will come no more. . . . and he arrived yesterday?' she coldly asks Suzuki. At her toneless 'Yes', Butterfly realises that the strange lady is Pinkerton's wife, who has come to take the child away from her. Calm and utterly composed, she turns to Kate and says she will give up the child to Pinkerton if he comes in half an hour to fetch him.

She has made up her mind to do away with herself. After Sharpless and Kate have left, she bids Suzuki to close the shutters so that the room is now in almost total darkness. She asks her about the child and is told by the maid that he is playing in another room. 'Let him play, and join him!' commands Butterfly, but the weeping Suzuki does not want to leave her and throws herself upon the ground, whereupon the geisha drags her to her feet and pushes her out of the room. Kneeling down before the image of the Buddha in silent prayer, she presently draws her father's dagger from its sheath and softly reads the inscription on it: 'To die with honour when one can no longer live with honour.' Just as she is pointing the dagger at her throat, Suzuki pushes the child into the room. Overcome by a mother's feeling, Butterfly drops the dagger and kisses the child passionately. Holding his face in her hands, she tells him why she is about to kill herself: 'You must never know that it is for you, for your dear innocent eyes that Butterfly dies, so that you may go away beyond the seas and not recall, when grown up, the mother who abandoned you. My son, sent to me from heaven, look straight into your mother's face so that a memory of it may linger. . . . Farewell, my dearest love!' (arietta: '*Tu! Tu! piccolo Iddio!*'). She seats the child on a stool with his face turned away from the screen and gives him a doll to play with,

OPPOSITE: *Yasuko Hayashi as Butterfly in the final scene*

43

while she gently bandages his eyes. She then seizes the dagger and, with her eyes fixed on the child, goes behind the screen. The knife is heard falling on to the ground and the white veil she had previously thrown over the screen disappears. Butterfly emerges and, tottering, she gropes her way towards the child, with the white veil now around her neck. She smiles feebly as she drags herself towards him and, with her remaining strength, embraces him; then falls to the ground beside him. Pinkerton's anxious cries 'Butterfly! Butterfly!' are heard from outside; the door is flung open and he and Sharpless rush in. The geisha weakly points to the child and dies. Pinkerton kneels beside her, while the Consul takes the child into his arms and kisses him.

The Music

By way of introduction to this chapter, something must be said about the general musical style of *Madam Butterfly*. Compared with Puccini's previous stage works, especially of the *tragédie larmoyante* type (*Manon Lescaut* and *La Bohème*), there is a heightened expressiveness and refinement in the lyrical writing and, generally, an added suppleness and plasticity in the melody and harmony. Puccini's characteristic technique of the mosaic—i.e., of ranging together a diversity of minute motifs into long phrases—seems particularly appropriate to an opera about little people and little things; there is, as it were, a symbolic relationship between the world of Butterfly and the tiny squares of Puccini's musical mosaic. Moreover, his use of the *leitmotif*, never strict in the Wagnerian sense, shows here a greater subtlety and pointedness in the delineation of Butterfly and in the reflection of her tragedy. A completely new aspect of the score is its exoticism, which wafts a strange alluring aroma over the greater part of the opera. Just as the heroine is inseparable from her particular *milieu*, so are the vivid exotic colours from her music. This was not mere *japonaiserie*, a mere veneer laid on from outside, but an integral part of Puccini's aim to create the atmosphere of the opera's peculiar setting. Yet, for all Puccini's extensive use of authentic (I was able to identify seven such original tunes) and quasi-authentic, 'imaginary' or 'self-made' Japanese melodies, of instrumental hues and timbres of an impressionist order, and of the pentatonic scale, the score of *Madam Butterfly* contains scarcely a bar that does not bear the composer's unmistakable signature. In other words, what strikes us as Japanese in this opera is Japanese as reflected in the prism of Puccini's imagination. But it must be added that he clearly distinguishes between East and West—the two Americans, Pinkerton and the Consul, are portrayed in what we may call Puccini's 'normal' style, while Butterfly and Suzuki, Goro and Yamadori are presented, as it were, in their native costumes; but at moments of lyrical effusion and exaltation the heroine casts off her exotic garment and dons a dress that would equally fit Manon and Mimì.

The opera opens with a brief orchestral introduction in which two ideas can be distinguished. The first is an animated theme, played *'vigorosamente'* and *'ruvidamente'* ('roughly'), and

RIGHT: *Manuscript page from the last act*

presented in the form of a strict four-part *fugato* (violins—violas—violoncellos—double-basses). (This fugal opening forcibly recalls the beginning of the overture to Smetana's *Bartered Bride*.) The second idea is a figure of four chords associated with Nagasaki, Butterfly's home town. Since the stress lies on the third chord, this motif may well have been inspired by the name Nagasaki with its emphasis on the third syllable. Both ideas occur frequently in Act I—the first, for instance, after Suzuki's evening prayer and during the love scene, and also during the scene of Goro's introduction to Pinkerton of Butterfly's three servants.

ABOVE: *Nagasaki in the 1860s, the time of the real incident on which* Madam Butterfly *is based*

ABOVE: *A Metropolitan Opera production with Renata Tebaldi (Butterfly), Barry Morell (Pinkerton) and Paul Franke (Goro), Act I*

Another idea of some importance is a (mainly) dotted theme in the character of a lively processional, first announced on the solo bassoon, [14], at the point when Goro enumerates the guests expected at Butterfly's wedding. As its subsequent use makes clear, the theme stands for the geisha's relatives and friends. With the arrival of the Consul—like Butterfly's, his voice is first heard offstage—the first violins play a four-bar strain which, in its lyrical expansion, is suggestive of this honest, good-hearted and altogether sympathetic character. As Sharpless contemplates the beautiful view of Nagasaki and Pinkerton explains to him his purchase of the house for 999 years, but with a monthly escape clause in the contract, the orchestra passes in review the nimble Japanese motifs and figures heard so far.

In a letter to Ricordi (23 April 1902), Puccini wrote that he was trying his best to make Pinkerton sing 'like an American'. In the event, the part of the naval lieutenant shows all the characteristics of a typically Puccinian tenor, with just a thin 'American' veneer spread over him. This comes out best in Pinkerton's aria '*Dovunque al mondo*' ('Wherever in the world'), which marks the change from Puccini's exotic manner to his normal 'western' style. To characterize Pinkerton in his capacity as naval officer, the composer (rather naïvely) opens the aria with the strains of 'The Star-Spangled Banner', scored in military-band fashion for woodwind and brass only. (One person, to be sure, objected strongly to Puccini's use of the American National Anthem—Gustave Kobbé of *Complete Opera Book* fame.) There is an air of breeziness, if not indeed

TOP LEFT: *Sena Jurinac as Butterfly during a rehearsal at Covent Garden in January 1950*

TOP RIGHT: *Hisako Hidaka and Hermann Esser in Act I of a Leipzig production*

brashness, about Pinkerton expounding to the Consul his easy-going view of life, not to mention the trivial realism of his offer of 'Milk-punch or Wisky' (sic) to Sharpless. But it is an effective piece, the lyricism of which is heightened by a markedly expressive *cantabile* phrase on the violoncellos, six bars after the opening, and repeated and expanded in the course of the aria. After some more exchanges between the two men, Pinkerton launches into a kind of arietta, '*Amore o grillo* ('Love or whim'), which sounds like the evocation of the graceful flutter of a butterfly, to which he likens his bride. There is even a description of fluttering wings in the clarinets and flute (four bars after [31]). Sharpless, recounting Butterfly's visit to the American Consulate and warning his friend not to hurt her trusting heart, is given gravely expressive music to sing, which returns shortly before the end of the opera. The arrival of Butterfly and her girl companions—their voices are first heard offstage—introduces the first moment of musical magic in the opera. Beginning with the chorus '*Quanto cielo! Quanto mar!*', an entrancingly beautiful motif is heard softly on the unmuted solo violin and solo viola (the rest of the strings play *con sordino*) and repeated (in sequence) several times; and this is followed immediately by a theme of flowing, lyrical character. Butterfly's 'Entrance' music, as it might be called, is so conceived as to suggest two different things—her tender and utterly lovable nature, and the wide expanse of sea and sky of which she sings as she climbs up the hill, an exquisite example, this, of Puccini's art of portraying in one and the same music a character and an atmosphere. As the party becomes visible—all carrying big umbrellas of gay colours and bowing before Pinkerton and the Consul—a most delightful theme is heard in a delicate orchestration for flute, oboe, harp and bells [41]. It is the first of the identifiable Japanese tunes that Puccini uses in the opera.

With the following exchanges between Butterfly, Sharpless and Pinkerton, the music returns to the light conversational style in which the opera began, a style first emerging in *La Bohème* and one of which Puccini, developing it from Verdi's *Falstaff*, became an unsurpassed modern master. In the scene in which the geisha hints at the misfortunes that have befallen her family, two ominous-sounding themes appear, both of which are, significantly, marked by the dissonant interval of the augmented fourth or tritone—the *diabolus in musica* of medieval

OPPOSITE: *Giuseppe Campora (Pinkerton) and Raina Kabaivanska (Butterfly) during the wedding ceremony, Act I. A New Orleans Opera production staged by Arthur Cosenza*

RIGHT: *Victoria de los Angeles and John Lanigan during a rehearsal for a Covent Garden performance in Spring 1957*

music. The first is heard in the vocal line in which the geisha refers to the poverty of her family—'*Nessuno si confessa mai. . .*' ('No one ever confesses . . .') [44], and the second, on the woodwind, occurs at the passage in which she says that 'even the strongest oaks will fall before a whirlwind' (four bars after [45]). The second idea seems to stand for Butterfly's premonition of her own sufferings, and will dominate the introduction to the orchestral Intermezzo leading to the second half of Act II. When Butterfly speaks of the necessity that forced her to become a geisha, namely, to earn her living, a sad melody in (largely) wholetones is thrown up by the orchestra (and repeated twice more five bars before [46]). An important theme of the opera which, at its first appearance, is made especially sinister by its dark colouring (low clarinets, bass clarinet and bassoon, three bars after [49]), is associated with her father's suicide, and in Act II foreshadows her own violent end. Goro's announcement of the arrival for the wedding ceremony of the two state officials is, appropriately, accompanied by the Japanese Imperial Hymn (strings). Then follows the gathering of Butterfly's relatives and friends to the tripping 'Relative' theme, and an animated ensemble develops in which the simultaneous chatter of different persons and groups (with a canon between the treble and lower voices) renders all their talk unintelligible—a clever device to create the effect of excited and noisy cross-talk. In the ensuing episode Sharpless and Pinkerton are given a beautifully-broad, lyrical melody, the Consul again warning his friend not to wound Butterfly's loving heart; at the same time, the relatives deliver themselves of unfavourable comments on the bridegroom, to a strongly rhythmic figure of pentatonic build. The way in which Puccini brings East and West together in this ensemble is masterly.

The following scene between Butterfly and Pinkerton is an exquisite 'conversation piece' in which she shows him the little knick-knacks she is bringing into the marriage, and in which another alluring Japanese tune, 'The Cherry Blossom', makes its appearance (solo oboe, five bars after [75]). As Butterfly pulls out of her sleeve a sheathed dagger, a strident figure, again marked by an augmented fourth, shoots up from violins and violas; this, too, will play an important role in Act II. As she speaks of her adoption of Pinkerton's faith, we hear a broadened version of the enchanting Japanese 'Bell' theme in a typically Puccinian unison of voice and strings, decked out with light, shimmering arpeggios on harp and woodwind.

Other composers might have inflated the wedding ceremony into a big spectacular scene, but Puccini, with his instinctive sense of style, dispatches it in a trice, the Imperial Commissioner reading the marriage contract in a dry, perfunctory voice, as is the habit of such officials. Butterfly's friends offer her, with repeated bows, their congratulations, to a fine, swaying melody derived from the Japanese song *The Ninon Bashi*. Encouraged by Pinkerton, they drink a toast to the bride and groom (chorus: '*O Kami! O Kami!*'), which is interrupted by furious offstage shouts of '*Cio-Cio-San! Abominazione!*'. It is the Uncle Bonze, who now appears, cursing Butterfly for having renounced her religion. At this moment [102] Puccini introduces a discordant wholetone figure, the 'Curse' motif, which has a particularly frightening effect. It is thundered out by the combined horns and trumpets, '*molto accentato*'. This motif henceforth symbolizes the geisha's ostracism by her family and her complete isolation in her own country. The crowd of relatives and friends, at first horror-stricken at the entry of the Bonze, now turn against her, shouting, '*Ti rinnegiamo!*' ('We renounce you!') and, to express their utter abhorrence of her, emit the Japanese word '*Hou!*' in a furious *portamento* (chromatic sliding of the voice). Driven away by Pinkerton, their shouts are heard with diminishing force from the distance, and will still echo into the following love scene.

Puccini, having established the atmosphere, delineated the main characters and exposed the drama, has cleared the decks for the lyrical second half of the act, which is occupied by the great love duet. For its wealth of ideas—Puccini poured at least six principal new themes into it— and for the suppleness and pliancy of the vocal parts, notably the heroine's, this duet ranks as perhaps the finest the composer ever penned. It is full of poetry—indeed, Illica considered that in this respect it surpasses the famous duet of Mimì and Rodolfo in Act I of *La Bohème*; it is, certainly, the most analytical in reflecting the finest shades of feeling and thought that invade the lovers' minds. For the time it lasts (thirteen to fourteen minutes) it may temper the revulsion the spectator feels for the cad Pinkerton (Ricordi called him a 'clyster'). As for the orchestra's part in this duet, it is most noteworthy for the infinite variety of colours and, almost for the first time since the opera's beginning, the warm, sensuous strings take full command of the situation. There is a profusion of markings in the score (*dolce, espressivo, cantando, sfumato, sfiorando, con sordino, sul tasto,* etc), and the lovers' growing rapture is mirrored in the gradually increasing sonorities of the orchestra, with four horns raising their bells (rare in Puccini) at the climax, '*È notte serena!*'. What with its richness of melody, diversity of rhythmic patterns, constant fluctuations in the level of dynamics and, lastly, its pervasive *tempo rubato* (all of which demands an unceasing flexibility and freedom of presentation from both the singers and the conductor), the music may give the impression of randomness. Yet a closer study of the duet lays bare a singularly controlled and cohesive structure, the outline of which is something like the following: From [111] to [116] there extends an introductory *arioso*, in which Pinkerton consoles and comforts the weeping Butterfly. The recall of previously heard themes and motifs here includes the sinister 'Curse' and the 'Suicide' of

LEFT: *Florence Easton who sang Butterfly at Covent Garden in 1909*

Butterfly's father, now softened in its impact through a full harmonization and the scoring for strings *divisi*. As Suzuki murmurs her evening prayer in Japanese, the fugal theme from the orchestral introduction to the act reappears. The actual love duet starts at '*Viene la sera*' [116], with a deeply felt upwards-leaping melody in the warm key of A major. There is a middle section, during which Butterfly changes into her night robe, so that the subsequent return of the opening results in a beautiful rounding-off of the little scene, in the form A–B–A. Tripartite, too, is the next section (three bars after [120] to one bar before [123]). There is an air of ineffable mystery in '*Somiglio la Dea della luna*' ('I am like the Moon Goddess'), and presently, at '*E li prende*' ('Then she takes them [the human hearts]'), the geisha breaks into a memorable phrase of six bars which leads back to a varied repeat of the opening strain. The third section is the most extensive [123–34]. It is so conceived as to form a so-called *Bogen* or arch, the fulcrum or key-stone of which rests on the portion beginning with Butterfly's most tender '*Vogliatemi bene*' ('Ah, love me a little' [128–31]) accompanied by a solo violin, *dolcissimo, espressivo*. After this, the music traces, so to speak, its step back to previous episodes, which is the essence of the arch form. Incidentally, it is here (one bar after [131]) that Butterfly speaks with prophetic irony of the westerner's practice of piercing the heart of a butterfly with a needle and fixing it on a board.

The great climax of the duet is its epilogue, which brings back the whole of Butterfly's 'Entrance' music, with the two lovers now joining together in overpowering rapture and working up to a final glorious close on the high C. As they make their way into the house, Puccini clinches the scene with a repeat of the Japanese 'Bell' theme scored for the wind only (*ff–pp*), and the curtain descends on a chord that sounds less like a conclusion than a question to which the future will provide the answer.

The second act, in which Butterfly's tragedy unfolds, represents Puccini's finest achievement in the psychological illumination of a character. The heroine's internal drama is mirrored in the music with a measure of insight and empathy the composer never surpassed. His inventive imagination and his feeling for style operate at full stretch, thus creating a musico-dramatic unity of compelling force.

It is three years since Pinkerton left Butterfly, yet her faith in his return is unshakable. But in the first of the four great scenes which make up Part 1 of Act II, she is depressed by thoughts of her isolation from her own people and of her approaching poverty. The mood of this opening scene is prepared by the short orchestral introduction, which takes the form of a miniature *fugato*. At the rise of the curtain, the 'Curse' motif (oboes, cor anglais and clarinets) is a pointed hint of what is passing through the geisha's mind as she sits on the floor, resting her head in her hands. Suzuki is crouching before an image of the Buddha and praying that *'Butterfly non pianga più!'* ('May Butterfly weep no more!'). Puccini sets her prayer, which she says in her own language, to a ritual tune of authentic origin. Its orchestration is a paradigm of the composer's instrumental exoticism: for nineteen bars the harmony never changes and Suzuki's pentatonic strain is embedded in a deep and monotonous sound (low clarinets, bass clarinet, muted horns, timpani, harp and upper strings); it perfectly fits the mood of the prayer. The first direct allusion to the tragedy comes in the insistent repeats of an extended version of the 'Suicide' theme, which accompanies the little episode in which Suzuki, counting the money Pinkerton left for paying the rent of the house, says that unless he returns soon they will fall on hard times, followed by Butterfly's raging fury at her maid's doubts that he will ever come back. *'Ah, taci o t'uccido!'* ('O, Silence or I'll kill you!'). Calming herself, she tells Suzuki what Pinkerton said to her on the day he left her—that he will return when the 'robins build their nest'. This little solo, beginning at [10], blossoms out into an entrancing pentatonic phrase, *'Butterfly, piccina mogliettina'* ('Dear little wife'), which recurs in the subsequent aria and which is clinched by an orchestral imitation of the gay twitter of birds. Taken aback by Suzuki's tears and accusing her of lack of faith, Butterfly now launches into a declaration of her unshakable conviction of Pinkerton's home-coming, in her famous aria, *'Un bel dì vedremo'* ('One fine day we'll see'), a most exquisite piece of music. She begins in a trance-like, visionary state of mind, imagining the sighting on the horizon of Pinkerton's ship, and picturing herself awaiting him on the hill, seeing him climb up and finally embracing her. The opening eight bars, a real *trouvaille*, are a gently undulating phrase built up of three tiny figures and may possibly have been inspired by the verbal image '*levarsi un filo di fumo*' ('a thread of smoke arising'). The vocal line is doubled by a clarinet and a solo violin, while the rest of the violins, playing with mutes, are to sound 'like a distant murmur'. It is a highly original example of Puccini's art of instrumentation. The middle section, beginning with '*Mi metto là*' [13], is an infinitely tender *arioso* containing a rising pentatonic phrase, '*S'avvia per la collina*' ('He climbs up the hill') that Puccini will use to shattering effect near the end of the opera. Presently the melodic figure originally set to '*Butterfly, piccina mogliettina!*' re-enters on the harp and two muted solo violins, thus underlining in its scoring the intimacy of the sentiment expressed by the heroine at this moment. This makes the return of the opening section, now *ff, con molta passione*, doubly effective. The final climax is reached at '*Tienti la tua paura, io con sicura fede l'aspetto*' ('You keep your fear, but I will expect him with firm faith') the last word being sung on the high B-flat. During the orchestral epilogue, Butterfly's tension subsides and the two women, deeply moved, embrace each other.

The next scene is perhaps the most important of the four, for in it Butterfly, who has up to now lived in a world of sweet dreams and illusions, is for the first time brought into contact with cruel reality, namely, the possibility that Pinkerton may never come back. The scene consists of three episodes of marked emotional and musical contrast. The first centres on Butterfly and the Consul, who has come with the purpose of acquainting her with the contents of a letter Pinkerton has sent to him. A conversational style prevails in the vocal parts, while the orchestra brings back previous material in pointed fashion. The principal new tune introduced into this episode is the 'Yamadori' theme, an authentic Japanese song, entitled 'My Prince'. But, strangely, at the point where we first hear it (the geisha offering Sharpless a pipe and 'American' cigarettes) we cannot by the widest stretch of the imagination bring it into any association with Yamadori. It is only when she refers to Goro's wanting to introduce her to a number of suitors, including a wealthy '*scimunito*' ('nincompoop') that we become aware that this jolly pentatonic strain stands for Yamadori.

The second episode is the visit of the Prince, whose pompous gait is suggested by the 'heavy' scoring of his theme for two bassoons, four horns and violoncellos, in unison. Butterfly addresses him in a long, expansive phrase full of yearning, that seems to be completely out of character with this figure of fun. An explanation for this discrepancy may be that Puccini wanted Butterfly to *simulate* the feelings Yamadori has for her, while at the same time showing her contempt for him by drawing out two syllables of his name YA—ma—DO—ri in a six-bar phrase (one bar after [29]). Again a few reminiscences are thrown in, among them the 'Star-spangled Banner', when the geisha speaks of '*mio paese, gli Stati Uniti*' ('my country, the United States'). The brief teaparty takes place to the tune of a *Valzer lentissimo* (English Waltz), the first instance in Puccini of the kind of elegant salon music that he was to write over a decade later in *La Rondine*, and one that here seems completely amiss. This was the only place in the opera that Puccini's assured sense of style deserted him.

BOTTOM LEFT: *Maggie Teyte in the title role at Covent Garden in 1937*

BOTTOM RIGHT: *Eva Turner as Butterfly in the 'Tea Party' scene, Act II (Covent Garden, c. 1920)*

The third episode opens with Sharpless's constantly frustrated attempts to read Pinkerton's letter to Butterfly. He manages, with interruptions by her, to get as far as the passage 'I ask you to prepare her carefully for the blow', but before he says the last word she interjects 'he returns', misses the word 'blow' and excitedly claps her hands. As the music to this 'Letter' scene recurs in Butterfly's night vigil, it will be discussed there, but here attention may be drawn to the remarkable transparency of the instrumental texture so as to enable the listener to follow the dialogue without difficulty. Butterfly's reaction to Sharpless's blunt question as to what she would do if Pinkerton never returned, is treated by Puccini with a minimum of means to achieve a maximum effect. A single note (A) is struck on the drum and the strings, *ff*, 'drily', a general pause, and Butterfly stands completely transformed 'as if struck by a death blow'. This duet of Butterfly and the Consul is in the character of those dirge-like processional marches of Puccini's which haunt the imagination (end of *La Bohème*, 'Execution' music of *Tosca*, Act III, and the March of the Condemned Princes in *Turandot*, Act I). With a suddenness characteristic of realistic opera, the spectator is catapulted into the scene in which Butterfly, struck by a new thought, rushes into the next room and fetches her child. We hear a triumphant version of the opening of her 'Entrance' music, followed by a new pentatonic figure which henceforth symbolizes her blond, blue-eyed son. Placing him on a cushion and kneeling beside him, she addresses to the boy the aria *'Che tua madre'* ('That your mother'). This is one of the opera's noblest inventions, cast in an unusual key (A-flat minor) and permeated by a feeling of unrelieved sadness. The aria has the character of both a funeral march and a dance song, with a heavy sarabande-like stress on the second beat of the bar. (The peculiar rhythmic pattern on which the music is based is already foreshadowed in Act I, in the conversation between Butterfly and the Consul, seven bars before [44]). Puccini obtains a singularly sinister effect at the phrase *'orribile destino, danzerà per te'* ('a horrible fate, the geisha will dance for you') when the strings play *col legno* a pentatonic figure which will recur in a *tutti* at the very end of the opera.

The third great scene of Part 1 again juxtaposes episodes of strong emotional contrast: Butterfly's blinding fury at Goro's spiteful remarks about her child's legitimacy, her repentance at

her sudden outburst, her tender thoughts for the child and her limitless joy at hearing the cannon shot announcing the arrival of Pinkerton's ship in the harbour—all accompanied by recalls of relevant previous material. Of these reminiscences, the one most likely to strike the listener is the repeat of the first sixteen bars of Butterfly's aria '*Un bel dì vedremo*', when she recognizes Pinkerton's ship; and, as she breaks into the jubilant phrase 'My love has triumphed', trumpets and woodwind intone the American National Anthem. The scene culminates in the 'Flower' duet, which released in Puccini a well of the most tender, lyrical music, music that seems to breathe the very fragrance of the flowers with which Butterfly and her maid now begin to adorn the room in preparation for Pinkerton's home-coming. Like the love duet of Act I, this duet has an elaborate form approaching a *rondo*. The main section [75], in which Puccini's treatment of the woodwind is particularly fine, reaches its climax in the lovely phrases beginning with '*Settiamo a mani piene*' ('Let us scatter in handfuls') with the two voices moving together in (mostly) euphonious thirds. The music has a gentle, dance-like lilt, as indeed the whole duet suggests the undulating movements of people strewing flowers on the ground.

The fourth and last scene of Part 1, centring on Butterfly's night vigil, begins with her preparation for it, when the orchestra reaches an expressive eloquence which, even without the words, tells us what is going on in her mind. As the geisha, together with her child and Suzuki, settles down to her vigil, the instruments break into an almost unbearably poignant phrase (five bars before [90]). Is it to convey the geisha's total isolation or to suggest something she does not yet know—the pathetic futility of her hopes?

In Belasco's play the *mise-en-scène* of the vigil was a sensation. Puccini's music turns it into one of the most poetic situations in all opera. This nocturne is as inspired a piece of music as ever sprang from the composer's head. It can be interpreted as a lullaby, suggesting the gradual falling asleep of Suzuki and the child. Above a gently rocking rhythmic ostinato on the three flutes and the muted strings, *pizz. ppp* (!), there rises a long wordless melody hummed by a chorus of sopranos and tenors in unison—a melody that has the simplicity and loveliness of a real folksong. (The choral tune is accompanied by a viola d'amore, offstage, introduced by Puccini, not to add a new instrumental colour but to ensure accurate intonation of the singers; the instrument is not to be heard in the auditorium.)

Part 2 of Act II is the shortest portion of the opera, and in the original version, to which many theatres are now returning, it followed without a break after the Humming Chorus. An orchestral Intermezzo is heard, expressing the thoughts and feelings which invade Butterfly as she stands against the *shosi*, staring out into the night and awaiting Pinkerton's home-coming; this Intermezzo is Puccini's most ambitious essay in symphonic writing. Sailors' calls ensue ('*Oh eh! Oh eh!*'), a passage that owes something to similar cries in Act I, Scene 3, of Debussy's *Pelléas et Mélisande*. This forms the transition to the 'Dawn' music, which in contrast to the Intermezzo is diatonic and simple of texture. (The stages of dawn-break to sunrise are marked in the score.)

With the awakening of Suzuki, who taps Butterfly on the shoulder, the action begins to move forward again. The brief scene until the geisha retires to rest in another room is dominated by the 'Child' figure. There is an admirable touch of delicacy in the little episode in which Butterfly says to the sleeping child, '*Dormi, amor mio*' ('Sleep, my love'), her words growing fainter and fainter as she disappears into the next room.

The arrival of Pinkerton and Sharpless is marked by the entry of an expressive threnodial theme, with grave processional steps in the bass, scored for strings only (*Largo*). When this *Largo* presently returns, a semitone lower, it starts as a solo for Sharpless, presently becoming a duet with Pinkerton and a trio

LEFT: *Rina Giacchetti and Giovanni Zenatello in an early Covent Garden production*

with Suzuki. It is in this trio that the part of the maid gains for the first time in musical importance. When Sharpless reminds Pinkerton of his warning at the wedding about Butterfly's trusting heart, he sings a literal repetition, even down to the same key, of the corresponding solo in Act I. Pinkerton, full of remorse at seeing the room in which he spent so many happy hours with the geisha, launches into his arietta '*Addio fiorito asil*'—'Farewell, beflowered place'. Both the trio and the arietta are concessions made by the dramatist to the musician, for they tend to retard the action. What they convey could have been got over in a few words of text. Moreover, the tenor's high A-flat and B-flat are calculated to awake Butterfly from her rest and bring her on to the scene forthwith, which is precisely what Pinkerton and the Consul wish to avoid. This is a striking example of how old operatic conventions were still strong enough for Puccini to allow them to obtrude in a realistic opera.

The following scene is largely in the composer's conversational style, and also shows the subtle psychological effects he extracts from his frequent use of rests and general pauses, as indeed the whole opera provides an instructive example of the application of this device.

The moment at which Suzuki tries to prevent Butterfly from entering the room is made terrifying by Puccini's ferocious orchestration—three trumpets, *ff, con tutta forza*, repeat three times a shortened version of the 'Curse' motif. By contrast, at the point at which Butterfly asks the maid to answer her question if Pinkerton is alive, by a simple 'Yes' or 'No', three solo violoncellos softly descend nearly a whole octave in wholetone steps, a passage that creates an indefinable *frisson*. And an extremely apt touch on the part of the composer and his two librettists in order to demonstrate Butterfly's immense natural dignity occurs in her conversation with Kate Pinkerton. (See the following chapter for changes and cuts in this scene.) To Kate's question, '*Potete perdonarmi?*' ('Can you forgive me?'), the geisha replies by wishing her all happiness and telling her not to be sad on her account. Her words '*Sotto il grande ponte del cielo . . .*' ('Under the great arc of Heaven . . .') are set to a phrase of outstanding lyrical beauty. In the subsequent scene where Butterfly, having made up her mind to end her life, drives Suzuki out of the room and then kneels before the image of the Buddha, there occurs an extraordinary passage of seventeen bars in which the two timpani hammer out a repeated fifth (B-flat–F) in a quick crescendo to *ff*, which is like the wild beating of a heart, subsiding again into *pp*. As the geisha takes her father's dagger from the shrine, the 'Suicide' theme is sounded 'roughly' on the low strings.

Puccini's librettists showed a high sense of drama when, just at the point where Butterfly is about to kill herself, they introduced a retarding element into the unbearable tension, by making Suzuki push the child into the room; Butterfly's subsequent farewell to the child thus arises *naturally* from the situation. '*Tu! tu! piccolo Iddio!*' is a most deeply felt arioso, in

BELOW: *Marie Collier as Butterfly (right) with Suzuki in Act I (Covent Garden, 1961)*

which Puccini introduces a succession of string chords plucked with the utmost force, 'almost in exaggeration', in order to indicate the mother's overwhelming emotion as she takes her child's head in her hands. The arioso culminates in a short arietta of no more than ten bars, '*O a me sceso dal trono . . .*' ('You, sent to me from Heaven . . .'), Puccini feeling that a full-length piece here would be out of place. This poignant farewell has all the characteristics of a true Puccinian *lamento*—a slow tempo, a minor key and falling fifths and fourths at phrase endings. As always in extreme situations, Puccini invents highly suggestive music for Butterfly's suicide. As she prepares for it, we hear on

RIGHT: *Renata Scotto as Butterfly (left) and Anna Maria Canali as Suzuki in Act II of a Florence production*

the low solo trumpet, *pp, tristamente*, a (syncopated) funereal *ostinato* above which the cor anglais and violas intone a *lamentoso* motif. This is followed by a much-shortened and varied version of her arietta, thus telling us that Butterfly's last thought before her self-immolation is for her child: a most subtle psychological touch in an opera that abounds in them. The exact moment at which she drives the dagger into her throat is indicated by a passage in which the combined woodwind, strings, horns and trumpet come crashing down, *ff*, on a single note (C-sharp), reinforced on the second beat of the bar by a harsh chord on trombones, bass trombones, timpani and double-bass, and, on the third beat, by a gong.

As Pinkerton is heard from behind the scene calling three times 'Butterfly!', the wholetone phrase from her first aria symbolizing his return is thundered out twice by three trumpets and three trombones in unison. The shattering irony of this passage is surpassed by what follows. As the dying Butterfly points with a weak gesture to the child, the whole orchestra blazes out, *tutta forza*, the dance rhythm of her second aria, '*Che tua madre*', in which, we recall, she says to the child the prophetic words that she would rather die than return to her profession of geisha. The insertion in the closing bar of the note G into the B minor tonality has the effect of a cataclysm.

The Original Version and Its Revisions

Much ado, we recall, was made by the critics of the Scala production of *Madam Butterfly* about the disproportionate length of the second act. This, it was argued, not only imposed great strain on Rosina Storchio, who was on the stage for practically the whole of its length, but was also an exacting test for the stamina of the Milan public of those days. For the Brescia production, three months later, Puccini divided the second act into two parts, with the curtain coming down after the Humming Chorus and raised again after the orchestral Intermezzo. Though the printed score keeps to this division, for many years the opera was given in three acts with two intervals, as I used to hear it at the Vienna Staatsoper during my student days in the middle 1920s. At some theatres a change was introduced, in that after the Humming Chorus the public remained in their seats and listened to the orchestral Intermezzo with the curtain down and the auditorium darkened. In England it was Rudolf Kempe who, during the 1955–6 season at Covent Garden, was the first to perform the second act as Puccini intended—i.e., undivided, with Butterfly's night vigil continuing on the open stage into the morning, when the action was resumed. This procedure has now been adopted by the English National Opera at the London Coliseum. Plainly, Puccini was ahead of his time when he had the idea of presenting Butterfly's actual drama in a single, uninterrupted act, as was the case with Belasco's play. Any argument based on the grounds that this would cause unnecessary mental fatigue to the interpreter of the title role and impose an undue strain on the audience is entirely invalidated by the success of long one-act operas such as Strauss's *Salome* and *Elektra* in which the heroine is on the stage virtually throughout.

There is, however, no doubt that the original version of the opera had defects and that the revisions made by the composer for Brescia and for Paris in 1906 are, with a few exceptions, a definite improvement. Anxious to reproduce an authentic Japanese atmosphere, Puccini crammed the first act with musical and scenic touches which appear wholly superfluous in the light of his later revisions. In developing the action, he put in too many minute details which, as one Italian critic put it, were suitable for a spoken drama but which, because of the generally retarding effect of *sung* music, slowed down the stage proceedings considerably. Thus, in the scene of the introduction of Butterfly's relatives to Pinkerton, Uncle Yakusidé had a little episode to himself, with his own music, designed to show him as a *beone* (a drunkard) and so heighten the comicality of the wedding party. Equally superfluous were the episodes of the naughty little boy of Butterfly's cousin, and of the relatives flinging themselves greedily on the refreshments offered them.

There is a set of cuts which were made, not in order to shorten musical scenes, but because tact and national susceptibilities demanded them; most of these excisions were textual ones

LEFT: *Costume design by Comelli for Yakusidé in the first English production at Covent Garden in July 1905*

and incorporated in the Paris production. In the original version, Pinkerton tells Goro that he will not call Butterfly's three servants by their proper names but 'Mug One—Mug Two—Mug Three'. Similarly, Pinkerton makes a sneering reference to Japanese gastronomic taste when he speaks of 'candied frogs and flies, birds' nests in syrup—the most nauseating tit-bit in Nippon', remarks which argue a surprising lack of tact and sensitivity on the part of Puccini and his librettists. Seen in this light, one appreciates Butterfly's words to Pinkerton in the original version, that when Goro suggested him to her as an eligible candidate for marriage she first recoiled from it because he was '*un americano, un barbaro*'. This sentence, in which the larger theme of the opera is hinted at, occurs in the cut of thirty-seven bars [124–6] in the love duet, a cut which would be worth opening. Indeed, the Pinkerton of the original version behaves with a degree of arrogance and overbearing associated with the white man in the days of colonization.

(Communism has seized on Pinkerton, as attested by a Bucharest production of *Madam Butterfly* in 1957 in which the writer of the programme book declared that the morals of the naval officer were those of the 'ruling Capitalist class in the United States'.) Incidentally, the changes to which Pinkerton's name and initials were subjected in the various editions make an amusing little story. 'B. F.' stands for Benjamin Franklin (what *else* could it stand for?), but in the cast list of the Italian scores he is called F. B. Pinkerton, while at the wedding ceremony the Imperial Commissioner names him 'Benjamin Franklin Pinkerton'. Much to the amusement of the Anglo-Saxon public, the cast list of an English edition has 'B. F.'! In the Italian edition of 1906, the ineluctable officer is knighted, with the name 'Sir Francis Blummy Pinkerton', as he is introduced by Sharpless to the Imperial Commissioner. Again, in the German edition his name is altered to F. B. Linkerton, the reason for which is not quite clear. Pinkerton was the name of a famous detective agency and is also the name of the hero of a series of thrillers which enjoyed great popularity in Central Europe at one time. It seems unlikely, however, that the change from P to L was due to these circumstances. Another, and perhaps more plausible, explanation is provided by the fact that in German the verb '*pinkeln*' is a vulgar expression for one of the body's daily functions.

In the second act the most notable musical revision was the addition to Pinkerton's part of the arietta, '*Addio, fiorito asil*'. Had Puccini followed Giacosa's argument that the tenor had not enough to sing in Act II, the arietta would, most probably, already have been in the first version. The 'Flower' duet was originally considerably longer than it is now, and so was the scene in which Butterfly prepares herself and her child for the night vigil. There was an entrancing episode showing Butterfly alternating between child-like, playful gaiety and sadness; moreover, she sings there a charming little lullaby, called by Puccini *Berceuse*, to the words '*Roje, un bimbo biondo*' ('Roje, a blond child').

The rest of the alterations in the second act were of a textual nature. Thus, Butterfly's second aria, '*Che tua madre*', had entirely different words from ten bars before [56], where the geisha describes a vision in which she sees the Mikado, surrounded by his army, make her son the most handsome

71

ABOVE: *Maggie Teyte (Butterfly) signing the marriage contract in a 1922 Covent Garden production*

RIGHT: *William Boland (Pinkerton) and Powell Edwards (Sharpless) singing the toast 'America for ever' (Covent Garden, 1922)*

prince of the realm. The new text, written for Paris, foreshadows Butterfly's tragic resolution of her moral conflict and is thus far more in keeping with the sad state of mind in which she sings the aria. There are some ten lines cut from her last scene with Suzuki and seven from her Farewell to the child, omitted, no doubt, in order to arrive at the *dénouement* with greater rapidity. Lastly, there is an important cut, as well as an alteration of the text, in the scene between Butterfly, Kate and the Consul. In the original version, Kate turns to the geisha and asks her to entrust the child to her care, just after Suzuki has told her mistress that Pinkerton will never come back. This was a piece of utter callousness on the part of the librettists, and Puccini himself felt uneasy about one word in particular. The word he objected to occurs in Kate's sentence, '*Io lo* terrei *con cura affetuosa*' ('I would care for him with great affection'). Writing to Giacosa (May 1903), he questions the verb '*terrei*' ('I would keep') and wants it to be replaced with something more gentle: 'I would say "I would hold him (in great affection), I would love him." But that "*terrei*", so hard, so cruel, hurts me.' Part of Kate's text was transferred to the Consul, the rest cut; and completely excised was the humiliating episode in which the Consul, acting on Pinkerton's instructions, offers Butterfly a sum of money as 'consolation', which she declines with great dignity.

To sum up. In the revisions made for Brescia and Paris, the first act was whittled down by no fewer than three hundred and sixty-two bars; the cuts in the second act amounted to considerably less. In the process, little of intrinsic musical interest was sacrificed (Yakusidé's music was feeble in any case) and most of what was jettisoned reappears in other portions of the score. There is little doubt that these revisions resulted in a tightening of the dramatic structure, and altogether contributed to an appreciable improvement of the score. In view of this, it is strange to learn that Puccini's publishers are preparing the original version for publication (evidently intended for performance). A compromise whereby certain material that was excised (such as parts from the love duet, the 'Flower' duet, and Butterfly's Lullaby) is incorporated in the revised version, would be of much greater advantage to the opera than a wholesale resurrection of the original.

Survey of Performances and Recordings

The cast for the Scala production of *Madam Butterfly* was hand-picked. All three principals—Rosina Storchio, Giovanni Zenatello (Pinkerton) and Giuseppe de Luca (Sharpless)—were in their prime and stood in the front rank of Italian opera singers. Moreover, all three belonged to the new school of 'actor-singers' which had emerged in response to the demands made on the performer by Italian realist opera. Instead of the rather stiff and static acting cultivated by older artists, their behaviour on the stage was dynamic, with lively, flexible gestures and movements. Outstanding in this respect was Storchio, a singer of high intelligence who had been discovered by Toscanini and whose overriding aim it was to place her fine and perfectly controlled soprano voice at the service of dramatic interpretation. Storchio was an ideal Butterfly, for she fully realized that mixture of child-like innocence, sincerity and credulity that characterizes this role. Butterfly's world is the world of illusions, and it was particularly this that Storchio conveyed with great conviction. Puccini spoke of her 'fine and delicate intelligence', and a Milan critic called her '*somma cantante e attrice*' ('supreme singer and actress'). There was irony in the fact that the Milan audience saw this eminent artist only once in a role which she performed with the greatest acclaim in Buenos Aires a few months later, and which she was to make her own.

The stage décor for the Scala production was by the noted French theatre painter Lucien Jusseaume, who, it seems, was also responsible for the stage designs of the Paris production in December 1906. The producer was Giulio Ricordi's eldest son, Tito, a man of dictatorial temperament, but highly intelligent and imaginative in his *mise-en-scène*. Yet he could not resist the temptation at the Milan performance to outdo Belasco in the scene of Butterfly's night vigil, for which he arranged a veritable bird concert to mark the break of dawn. Tito Ricordi was

74

responsible for a tour of *Madam Butterfly* through a number of American cities in 1906–7, said to have been the first venture of its kind. In collaboration with Belasco, he produced the first performance, too, of Puccini's *La Fanciulla del West* in New York in December 1910.

Puccini was anxious that the opera be given in Paris at the first opportunity, as he considered the French capital next in importance to Milan in the world of opera. It was staged there in December 1906 by Albert Carré, the director of the Opéra Comique and husband of the first French Butterfly, Marguerite Giraud. For the production, we recall, Puccini made new and mainly textual changes, an operation which, in Ricordi's eyes, lowered the composer's dignity.

The first Covent Garden production was mounted on 10 July 1905, with a cast that represented a rare constellation of stars of the first magnitude: Emmy Destinn, who became London's

BELOW: *Act II in a Metropolitan Opera production of 1907–8. Helen Mapleson (Kate), Louise Homer (Suzuki) and Geraldine Farrar (Butterfly)*

favourite interpreter of the title role; Enrico Caruso; and Antonio Scotti, one of the leading baritones of his day. The same cast also sang in the summer seasons of 1906 and 1913.

In the autumn of 1905, Rina Giachetti was Cio-Cio-San, partnered by Zenatello, Puccini's first Pinkerton. The conductor on this occasion was Leopoldo Mugnone, a fine Puccinian interpreter, who had directed *La Bohème* to its triumph at Palermo in 1896 and whom Beecham considered one of the best Italian conductors of the time. In the summer season of 1906 there were two outstanding Butterflys who alternated with each other—Destinn and Giachetti. The 1907 season was opened with *Madam Butterfly*, with Giuseppe de Luca as Sharpless. As three years before, at La Scala, De Luca appeared extravagantly costumed and wearing a monocle, for which he was much criticized; but he impressed by his pure though not large voice and his vivid acting. In the winter 1909 season, Florence Easton sang Cio-Cio-San, and was much praised for her beautiful, bell-like voice and excellent diction. At the end of the 'Entrance' music, she took the high D-flat instead of the B-flat (both versions are printed in the score), which no soprano had attempted before. In the summer of 1912, John McCormack sang Pinkerton for the first time.

After World War I there was a *Butterfly* revival at Covent Garden virtually every season. In the summer of 1919 Destinn (or Destinnova, as she wished to be known after Czechoslovakia had achieved independence) came back, with Giovanni Martinelli as Pinkerton and Dinh Gilly, a noted Algiers-born French baritone, as Sharpless. A performance in the 1920–21 season (12 May) was noteworthy for its trilingual aspect—Gilda dalla Rizza sang in Italian, Joseph Hislop in Swedish (!) and Gilly in English. During that same season, Maggie Teyte made her *début* as Butterfly, a success that she repeated in 1922.

During the Carl Rosa season at Covent Garden, from 1920–22, Eva Turner sang Cio-Cio-San for the first time. It was in this role that an Italian conductor heard her at the Scala Theatre in the 1924–5 season and told her to go to Milan for an audition with Toscanini; and it was in this way that her great international career began. In the International Grand Season at Covent Garden from May to July 1925, the Irish-born singer Margaret Sheridan appeared in the title role, wearing the costumes that had once belonged to Rosina Storchio. Though

on this occasion opinions on her singing were divided, the general verdict in subsequent years was that Butterfly was her best role. The final performance of this season brought to Covent Garden a German singer, Elisabeth Rethberg, who received great acclaim. During the 1928 summer season, Rosetta Pampanini made her *début* as Butterfly, winning golden opinions for the dramatic quality of her voice, and another excellent interpreter of the part was Dusolina Giannini. Towards the end of this season (30 June) a popular Saturday night performance of *Madam Butterfly* saw a young and highly talented musician on the conductor's rostrum—John Barbirolli. In 1930 Sheridan and Teyte were heard again. There was an interval of six years before *Madam Butterfly* came back into the repertoire of Covent Garden, when Teyte was partnered by a new Pinkerton—Heddle Nash, who was to become much in demand.

The post-war season in 1946 opened with a visit by the San Carlo Opera, Naples, with Onelia Fineschi in the title role. 1947 saw the foundation of the Covent Garden Opera Company, which in the 1949–50 season engaged Elisabeth Schwarzkopf as Cio-Cio-San. She sang with her accustomed artistry, but was

ABOVE: *Virginia Zeani (Butterfly) and Giangiacomo Guelfi (Sharpless) in a 1965–66 Scala production*

TOP LEFT: *Emmy Destinn who sang Butterfly at the first English production at Covent Garden in July 1905*

TOP RIGHT: *Butterfly (Anna Moffo) arriving at the house on the hill in Act I. A Milan Studio TV production (January 1956)*

found to be lacking in tenderness and sensitivity. On this occasion Monica Sinclair, who was to become one of the Company's most useful members, was an outstanding Suzuki. This production was staged with much taste and discretion by the choreographer Robert Helpmann. A year later Victoria de los Angeles gave an accomplished account of the part, greatly impressing the audience by her natural response to its emotional demands and by her vocal performance. In the 1955–6 season, Rudolf Kempe was in charge of Covent Garden, when he introduced for the first time Puccini's original version of the second act, which came as a revelation to both public and critics. Amy Shuard sang the title role. Los Angeles made a welcome return to the part in April and May 1957, when she was partnered by John Lanigan and Geraint Evans. The conductor was again Kempe. The opera was sung in Italian, which marked a new departure in policy, for foreign guest artists were thus enabled to sing their famous roles with members of the English company. The era of bi- and tri-lingual performances had passed for ever. Up to now, other interpreters of Butterfly have included Sena Jurinac, Renata Scotto, Marie Collier, Elizabeth Vaughan and Yasuko Hayashi. It should be added that during his lifetime Puccini disliked Japanese singers, whom he dismissed as 'those gramophone voices'. But this was before 1925 when electric recording was first introduced.

In the first performance at the Metropolitan Opera, New York, on 11 February, 1907, Geraldine Farrar, Enrico Caruso

BELOW: Butterfly (Schwarzkopf) is prevented by Suzuki (Sinclair) from killing Goro (David Tree) for spreading false rumours about her child's legitimacy (Covent Garden, 1950)

ABOVE: *Renata Scotto (Butterfly) in the 'Letter' scene with Robert Savoie (Sharpless) at Covent Garden in 1963*

and Antonio Scotti sang the leading roles, with Louise Homer as Suzuki. Later, Emmy Destinn was heard as Butterfly. Other popular interpreters of the title-role at the Met have included Elisabeth Rethberg, Licia Albanese, Dorothy Kirsten and Victoria de los Angeles. Leontyne Price first sang Butterfly during the 1961–2 season.

A Note On Recordings

The earliest complete recording of the opera on LP was issued by Decca in 1952: Renata Tebaldi was a full-voiced Cio-Cio-San and Giuseppe Campora an excellent Pinkerton. The baritone Giuseppe Inghilleri, nearing the end of a distinguished career, sang Sharpless, and Alberto Erede conducted. But three years later HMV offered a far superior performance from a much more interesting conductor, Gianandrea Gavazzeni, with a very strong cast of principals. As Butterfly, Victoria de los Angeles sounded less mature than Tebaldi. Her voice, then in its prime, was absolutely beautiful, and her characterization of the role was intelligent and detailed without being in the slightest degree self-conscious: 'profuse strains of unpremeditated art', it seemed. Giuseppe di Stefano presented a Pinkerton in the old, swaggering Gigli manner, and the role can take this kind of approach (or non-approach). The strong personality and highly

BELOW: *Mildred Miller as Suzuki and Leontyne Price as Butterfly in a Lyric Opera of Chicago production, 1960*

individual timbre of Tito Gobbi made much of Sharpless.

In 1956, a year after the Victoria de los Angeles *Butterfly*, Callas entered the lists with her portrayal of the role. But this was never one of Callas's best roles, and on disc she sounded far too bossy a Butterfly, ill-suited for pairing with the ardent, noble Pinkerton of the young Nicolai Gedda. Mario Boriello was Sharpless, and Karajan conducted somewhat clinically, his tempi inclined towards slowness. In the late fifties Tebaldi returned to the role. Though hardly qualifying as even an attempt at characterization, her Butterfly was gloriously sung: for her admirers this was all that mattered. Carlo Bergonzi offered a tastefully sung Pinkerton, Enzo Sordello a dull Sharpless, and Tullio Serafin conducted the Santa Cecilia forces

RIGHT: *Renata Tebaldi (Butterfly) and Giuseppe Di Stefano (Pinkerton) in the love duet of Act I (Lyric Opera of Chicago, October 1958)*

OPPOSITE: *Sena Jurinac and Charles Craig during a rehearsal at Covent Garden on 12 January 1959*

in a performance of marvellous warmth and authority.

At this point, an old recording from the days of 78s surfaced on LP, with a cast of favourite singers from the thirties. Toti dal Monte was a most convincing Butterfly, Gigli was heard at his best, and Mario Basiola, one of the finest Italian baritones of his day, was well in the picture as Sharpless. Oliviero de Fabritiis was the dependable conductor. In the 1960s, several more new recordings appeared. The first of them came from HMV, with Victoria de los Angeles returning to the title-role, in an even more moving performance than before, and this time with a tenor really worthy of her, Jussi Björling, and a personable Sharpless in Mario Sereni. Gabriele Santini conducted adequately. Then RCA issued a *Butterfly* with the creamy voice of Leontyne Price as Cio-Cio-San: a carefully thought-out interpretation. Pinkerton was Richard Tucker in one of his less stylish performances, and Leinsdorf offered anything but a routine account of the score.

In the late sixties, HMV produced a recording to rival their de los Angeles-Björling version. Renata Scotto was a Butterfly in the Toti dal Monte tradition, Carlo Bergonzi repeated his finely sung Pinkerton (heard earlier with Tebaldi), and Rolando Panerai made a telling and sympathetic figure of the consul. A performance of great warmth and stature was conducted by Sir John Barbirolli. A version from 78s, featuring Eleanor Steber, Richard Tucker and Giuseppe Valdengo, with the Metropolitan Opera Orchestra under Max Rudolf (originally recorded in 1947) was a useful souvenir of Met performances of the forties, with Steber an unusually robust Butterfly.

Herbert von Karajan returned to the opera in the mid-seventies with a sumptuously played and sung performance, in which the Vienna Philharmonic are heard to marvellous effect. They and Karajan make parts of the opera sound like Mahler! Mirella Freni, whose career reached new heights under Karajan, was a superb Butterfly and, though Luciano Pavarotti was more Italian tenor than American naval Lieutenant, he sounded magnificent. Robert Kerns made a somewhat pallid Sharpless, but Christa Ludwig as Suzuki almost stole the show.

A Decca recording with Montserrat Caballé is one of the least satisfactory performances of the opera on record. Caballé makes lovely sounds, but she is grossly miscast in a role in which she would be unlikely to be successful on stage. The other singers,

OPPOSITE: *Plácido Domingo and Francesca Roberto with Kay Creed as Suzuki in a production of the New York City Opera*

85

among them the soprano's husband as Pinkerton, are in-adequate, and the conductor (Armando Gatto) is more obedient to his prima donna than to his composer. Much better is a CBS recording in 1978 with Renata Scotto returning to the title-role, her voice now hardening at the top but her grasp of the character even surer than when she last recorded the role. Plácido Domingo is his usual anonymous self as Pinkerton: a fine voice but a dull musical personality. Ingvar Wixell makes much of Sharpless, a role which is a gift to a middle-aged baritone who can act, and Lorin Maazel, while lacking the easy authority of a Serafin or the personality of Karajan or Barbirolli, conducts an excellent performance.

C.O.

Libretto

TIME: THE EARLY 1900S
PLACE: JAPAN

English translation by Charles Osborne

ATTO PRIMO

Collina presso Nagasaki. Casa giapponese, terrazza e giardino. In fondo, al basso, la rada, il porto, la città di Nagasaki.

PINKERTON

E soffitto e pareti . . .

GORO

Vanno e vengono a prova,
a norma che vi giova
nello stesso locale alternar
nuovi aspetti ai consueti.

PINKERTON

Il nido nuzial dov'è?

GORO

Qui, o là . . . secondo . . .

PINKERTON

Anch'esso a doppio fondo! La sala?

GORO

Ecco!

PINKERTON

All'aperto?

GORO

Un fianco scorre . . .

PINKERTON

Capisco! capisco! Un altro . . .

ACT I

A hill near Nagasaki. A Japanese house, terrace and garden. In the background, at the bottom of the hill, the roads, harbour and city of Nagasaki.

PINKERTON

And the ceilings and walls . . .

GORO

Slide back and forth at will,
so that you can enjoy
from one and the same spot
ever-changing vistas.

PINKERTON

Where is the bridal chamber?

GORO

Here, or there . . . it depends . . .

PINKERTON

This, too, has sliding walls! The lounge?

GORO

This is it!

PINKERTON

In the open air?

GORO

One side slides out . . .

PINKERTON

I see! I see! Another . . .

GORO

Scivola!

GORO

Glides out!

PINKERTON

E la dimora frivola . . .

PINKERTON

And this insubstantial dwelling . . .

GORO

Salda come una torre,
da terra fino al tetto.

GORO

As steady as a tower,
from floor to ceiling.

PINKERTON

È una casa a soffietto.

PINKERTON

. . . is extremely delicate.

GORO

Questa è la cameriera
che della vostra sposa
fu già serva amorosa.
Il cuoco . . . il servitore.
Son confusi
del grande onore.

GORO

This is the chambermaid
who is already your bride's
devoted maid.
The cook . . . the manservant.
They are confused
by this great honour.

PINKERTON

I nomi?

PINKERTON

Their names?

GORO

Miss Nuvola leggiera,
Raggio di sol nascente,
Esala aromi.

GORO

Miss Light Cloud,
Ray of the Rising Sun,
Scented Breath.

SUZUKI

Sorride Vostro Onore?
Il riso è frutto e fiore.
Disse il savio Ocunama:
dei crucci la trama
smaglia il sorriso.
Schiude alla perla il guscio,
apre all'uomo l'uscio
del Paradiso.
Profumo degli Dei,
fontana della vita . . .

SUZUKI

My lord is pleased to smile?
A smile is a fruit and a flower.
The wise Ocunama said:
a smile breaks through
a web of trouble.
It opens the shell for the pearl,
it opens the gates
of Paradise to man.
The perfume of the gods,
the fountain of life . . .

Disse il savio Ocunama:
dei crucci la trama
smaglia il sorriso.

The wise Ocunama said:
a smile breaks through
a web of trouble.

PINKERTON

A chiacchiere costei mi par
cosmopolita.
Che guardi?

PINKERTON

Her chattering is just like women
the whole world over.
What are you looking at?

GORO

Se non giunge ancor la sposa.

GORO

To see if the bride's coming.

PINKERTON

Tutto è pronto?

PINKERTON

Is everything ready?

GORO

Ogni cosa.

GORO

Everything.

PINKERTON

Gran perla di sensale!

PINKERTON

What a gem of a marriage broker!

GORO

Qui verran: l'Ufficiale del registro,
i parenti, il vostro Console, la fidanzata.
Qui si firma l'atto
e il matrimonio è fatto.

GORO

The registrar, the relatives, your Consul
and the bride will all come.
You'll sign the contract here
and you'll be married.

PINKERTON

E son molti i parenti?

PINKERTON

Are there many relatives?

GORO

La suocera, la nonna,
Io zio Bonzo
(che non ci degnerà di sua presenza),
e cugini, e le cugine . . .
Mettiam fra gli ascendenti
ed i collaterali un due dozzine.
Quanto alla discendenza,
provvederanno assai
Vostra Grazia e la bella Butterfly.

GORO

The mother-in-law, the grandmother,
her uncle, the Bonze
(who won't honour us with his
presence),
and all the cousins male and female.
What with the old generation and
contemporaries
it comes to about a couple of dozen.
As for descendants,
your Honour and the beautiful Butterfly
will be sure to take care of that.

PINKERTON

Gran perla di sensale!

SHARPLESS

E suda e arrampica!
sbuffa, inciampica!

GORO

Il Consol sale.

SHARPLESS

Ah! quei ciottoli mi hanno sfiaccato!

PINKERTON

Bene arrivato.

GORO

Bene arrivato.

SHARPLESS

Ouff!

PINKERTON

Presto, Goro, qualche ristoro.

SHARPLESS

Alto.

PINKERTON

Ma bello!

SHARPLESS

Nagasaki, il mare, il porto . . .

PINKERTON

E una casetta
che obbedisce a bacchetta.

SHARPLESS

Vostra?

PINKERTON

What a gem of a marriage broker!

SHARPLESS

One sweats and scrambles,
puffs and stumbles!

GORO

The Consul's coming up.

SHARPLESS

Oh those stones have worn me out!

PINKERTON

Welcome.

GORO

Welcome.

SHARPLESS

Phew!

PINKERTON

Quickly, Goro, some refreshment.

SHARPLESS

What a height!

PINKERTON

But lovely!

SHARPLESS

Nagasaki, the sea, the harbour . . .

PINKERTON

And a little house
that responds to the wave of a wand.

SHARPLESS

Yours?

PINKERTON

La comperai per novecento
novantanove anni,
con facoltà, ogni mese,
di rescinder i patti.
Son in questo paese
elastici del par, case e contratti.

SHARPLESS

E l'uomo esperto ne profitta.

PINKERTON

Certo.
Dovunque al mondo
lo Yankee vagabondo
si gode e traffica
sprezzando i rischi.
Affonda l'àncora alla ventura, . . .
Milk-punch, o whisky?
. . . affonda l'àncora alla ventura,
finchè una raffica scompigli nave
e ormeggi, alberatura.
La vita ei non appaga
se non fa suo tesor
i fiori d'ogni plaga, . . .

SHARPLESS

È un facile vangelo.

PINKERTON

. . . d'ogni bella gli amor.

SHARPLESS

È un facile vengelo
che fa la vita vaga,
ma che intristisce il cor.

PINKERTON

Vinto si tuffa, la sorte riacciuffa.
Il suo talento
fa in ogni dove.
Così mi sposo all'uso giapponese

PINKERTON

I've bought it for nine hundred
and ninety-nine years,
with the option, every month,
to cancel the agreement.
In this country houses
and contracts are equally elastic.

SHARPLESS

And the clever man profits by it.

PINKERTON

Certainly.
All over the world
the vagabond Yankee
enjoys himself and takes his profit
ignoring all risks.
He drops anchor at random . . .
Milk-punch or whisky?
. . . he drops anchor at random
until a squall wrecks the ship,
moorings, rigging and all.
He's not content with life
unless he can find enjoyment
in every place he visits. . .

SHARPLESS

That's an easy creed.

PINKERTON

. . . and win the love of every pretty
girl.

SHARPLESS

An easy creed
which makes life delightful,
but saddens the heart.

PINKERTON

If he's beaten, he tries his luck again;
he pleases himself
wherever he goes.
So I'm marrying Japanese style,

per novecento
novantanove
anni.
Salvo a prosciogliermi ogni mese.

SHARPLESS

È un facile vangelo.

PINKERTON

America for ever!

SHARPLESS

America for ever! . . .
Ed è bella la sposa?

GORO

Una ghirlanda di fiori freschi,
una stella dai raggi d'oro . . .
E per nulla: sol cento yen.

Se Vostra Grazia mi comanda
ce n'ho un assortimento.

PINKERTON

Va, conducila, Goro.

SHARPLESS

Quale smania vi prende!
Sareste addirittura
cotto?

PINKERTON

Non so! Non so! Dipende
dal grado di cottura!
Amore o grillo, dir non saprei.
Certo costei
m'ha coll'ingenue arti invescato.

Lieve qual tenue vetro soffiato
alla statura, al portamento

for nine hundred
and ninety-nine
years,
with the right every month to break it
off.

SHARPLESS

It's an easy creed.

PINKERTON

America for ever!

SHARPLESS

America for ever! . . .
And is the bride pretty?

GORO

A garland of fresh flowers,
a star with golden rays . . .
And for a mere nothing: only one
hundred yen.
If your Grace commands,
I have a large assortment.

PINKERTON

Go and fetch her, Goro.

SHARPLESS

What madness has seized you!
Are you completely
infatuated?

PINKERTON

I don't know! I don't know! It depends
what you mean by infatuation!
Love or fancy, I couldn't say.
All I know is she's
bewitched me with her ingenuous
manner.
Light and slender as a piece of blown
glass

sembra figura da paravento.
Ma dal suo lucido fondo di lacca
come con subito moto si stacca,
qual farfalletta svolazza e posa
con tal grazietta silenziosa
che di rincorrerla furor m'assale,
se pure infrangerne dovessi l'ale.

in stature, in bearing
she's like a figure on a painted screen.
But from her glittering background of
lacquer,
with a sudden movement she frees
herself,
flutters like a butterfly and comes to rest
with such silent grace that a sudden
desire
seizes me to pursue her,
though I may crush her wings.

SHARPLESS

Ier l'altro, il Consolato
sen venne a visitar.
Io non la vidi,
ma l'udii parlar.
Di sua voce il mistero
l'anima mi colpì.
Certo quando è sincer
l'amor parla così.
Sarebbe gran peccato
le lievi ali strappar
e desolar forse un credulo cor.

SHARPLESS

The other day she paid
a visit to the Consulate.
I didn't see her,
but I heard her speaking.
The mystery of her voice
touched my heart.
I'm sure that true love
must speak like that.
It would be a great sin
to strip off those delicate wings
and perhaps grieve a trusting heart.

PINKERTON

Console mio garbato, quetatevi!
Si sa, . . .

PINKERTON

My dear Consul, calm down!
I know . . .

SHARPLESS

Sarebbe gran peccato.

SHARPLESS

It would be a great sin.

PINKERTON

. . . la vostra età è di flebile umor . . .

. . . Non c'è gran male s'io vo'
quell'ale . . .

PINKERTON

. . . that at your age one tends to be
sad. . .
No great harm is done if I'd like
those wings . . .

SHARPLESS

Quella divina mite vocina . . .

SHARPLESS

That divine, sweet little voice . . .

PINKERTON

. . . drizzar ai dolci voli dell'amor!

PINKERTON

. . . to spread themselves in a sweet
flight of love!

94

SHARPLESS

. . . non dovrebbe dar note di dolor!

PINKERTON

Whisky?

SHARPLESS

Un'altro bicchiere.
Bevo alla vostra famiglia lontana.

PINKERTON

E al giorno in cui mi sposerò con vere
nozze a una vera sposa americana.

AMICHE DI BUTTERFLY

Ah!

GORO

Ecco! Son giunte al sommo del pendio.

Già del femmineo sciame
qual di vento in fogliame
s'ode il brusio!

AMICHE

Ah! Ah! Ah! Ah!
Ah! Quanto cielo! Quanto mar!

BUTTERFLY

Ancora un passo or via . . .

AMICHE

Come sei tarda!

BUTTERFLY

Aspetta.

AMICHE

Ecco la vetta.
Guarda, guarda quanti fior!

SHARPLESS

. . . should not utter notes of sorrow!

PINKERTON

Whisky?

SHARPLESS

Another glass.
I drink to your family far away.

PINKERTON

And to the day when, in a real
ceremony, I marry a real American
bride.

BUTTERFLY'S FRIENDS

Ah!

GORO

Here they are! They've reached the top
of the hill.
Already you can hear the swarm
of women, like leaves
rustling in the wind.

FRIENDS

Ah! Ah! Ah! Ah!
Ah! So much expanse of sky! So wide a
sea!

BUTTERFLY

One more step to go . . .

FRIENDS

How slow you are!

BUTTERFLY

Wait.

FRIENDS

Here is the summit.
Look at all the flowers!

BUTTERFLY

Spira sul mare e sulla terra . . .

AMICHE

Quanto cielo! Quanto mar!

BUTTERFLY

. . . un primaveril . . .
. . . soffio giocondo.

SHARPLESS

O allegro cinguettar di gioventù!

BUTTERFLY

Io sono la fanciulla . . .
. . . più lieta del Giappone, . . .

AMICHE

Quanti fior! Quanto mar!

BUTTERFLY

. . . anzi del mondo. Amiche, io son
venuta . . .

AMICHE

Quanto cielo! Quanti fior!

BUTTERFLY

. . . al richiamo . . .
. . . d'amor, d'amor venni alle
soglie . . .

AMICHE

Gioia a te, gioia a te sia, dolce
amica, . . .

BUTTERFLY

. . .ove . . .

BUTTERFLY

Over the land and the sea there
floats . . .

FRIENDS

So much expanse of sky! So wide a sea!

BUTTERFLY

. . . a joyous . . .
. . . breath of spring.

SHARPLESS

Ah, youth's happy chatter!

BUTTERFLY

I am the happiest . . .
. . . girl in Japan . . .

FRIENDS

So many flowers! So wide a sea!

BUTTERFLY

. . . indeed, in the world. Friends, I have
come . . .

FRIENDS

So much expanse of sky! So many
flowers!

BUTTERFLY

. . . at the call . . .
. . . of love, I am come to the threshold
of love . . .

FRIENDS

Joy to you, joy to you, sweet
friend . . .

BUTTERFLY

. . . where . . .

AMICHE

. . . ma pria di varcar . . .

BUTTERFLY

. . . s'accoglie il bene di chi vive e di
chi muor.

AMICHE

. . . la soglia che t'attira, volgiti e
mira
le cose che ti son care, . . .
. . . mira quanto cielo, quanti fiori,
quanto mar!

BUTTERFLY

Amiche, . . .
. . . io son venuta al richiamo d'amor,
etc.

AMICHE

Gioia a te, *etc.*

BUTTERFLY

Siam giunte.
F. B. Pinkerton. Giù!

AMICHE

Giù.

BUTTERFLY

Gran ventura.

AMICHE

Riverenza.

PINKERTON

È un po' dura la scalata?

BUTTERFLY

A una sposa costumata
più penosa è l'impazienza.

FRIENDS

. . . but before you cross . . .

BUTTERFLY

. . . is gathered the happiness of those
who live and those who die.

FRIENDS

. . . the threshold which invites you,
turn and look
at those things which are dear to
you, . . .
. . . look at all this expanse of sky
and flowers and sea!

BUTTERFLY

Friends, . . .
. . .I have come at the call of love,
etc.

FRIENDS

Joy to you, etc.

BUTTERFLY

We are here.
F. B. Pinkerton. Down!

FRIENDS

Down.

BUTTERFLY

Good fortune attend you.

FRIENDS

At your service.

PINKERTON

Was the climb rather hard?

BUTTERFLY

To a well-mannered bride,
impatience is more painful.

PINKERTON

Molto raro complimento.

BUTTERFLY

Dei più belli ancor ne so.

PINKERTON

Dei gioelli!

BUTTERFLY

Se vi è caro, sul momento . . .

PINKERTON

Grazie, no.

SHARPLESS

Miss Butterfly. Bel nome,
vi sta a meraviglia.
Siete di Nagasaki?

BUTTERFLY

Signor sì. Di famiglia
assai prospera un tempo.
Verità?

AMICHE

Verità!

BUTTERFLY

Nessuno si confessa mai
nato in povertâ,
non c'è vagabondo
che a sentirlo non sia
di gran prosapia.
Eppur connobbi la ricchezza.
Ma il turbine rovescia
le quercie più robuste . . .
e abbiam fatto la ghescia
per sostentarci. Vero?

AMICHE

Vero!

PINKERTON

A very pretty compliment.

BUTTERFLY

I know some even prettier ones.

PINKERTON

Such jewels they must be!

BUTTERFLY

If you'd like some now. . .

PINKERTON

Thank you, no.

SHARPLESS

Miss Butterfly . . . A lovely name—
it suits you marvellously.
Are you from Nagasaki?

BUTTERFLY

Yes, sir. From a family
which was once quite well-to-do.
Is that not true?

FRIENDS

That is true!

BUTTERFLY

Nobody ever confesses
to having been born in poverty.
There isn't a beggar
who wouldn't tell you
he came from a noble family.
All the same, I have known wealth,
but the whirlwind uproots
the sturdiest oak . . .
and we became geishas
to support ourselves. Isn't that true?

FRIENDS

That's true!

BUTTERFLY

Non lo nascondo, nè m'adonto.
Ridete? Perchè?'Cose del mondo.

PINKERTON

Con quel fare di bambola,
quando parla m'infiamma.

SHARPLESS

Ed avete sorelle?

BUTTERFLY

No signore. Ho la mamma.

GORO

Una nobile dama.

BUTTERFLY

Ma, senza farle torto,
povera molto anch'essa.

SHARPLESS

E vosto padre?

BUTTERFLY

Morto.

SHARPLESS

Quant'anni avete?

BUTTERFLY

Indovinate.

SHARPLESS

Dieci.

BUTTERFLY

Crescete.

BUTTERFLY

I don't hide it, nor am I ashamed of it.
You laugh? Why? The world is like
that.

PINKERTON

With those child-like ways,
when she talks, I'm on fire.

SHARPLESS

And have you any sisters?

BUTTERFLY

No, sir. I have my mother.

GORO

A noble lady.

BUTTERFLY

But, without wishing to wrong her,
very poor, too.

SHARPLESS

And your father?

BUTTERFLY

Dead.

SHARPLESS

How old are you?

BUTTERFLY

Guess.

SHARPLESS

Ten.

BUTTERFLY

Higher.

SHARPLESS

Venti.

BUTTERFLY

Calate.
Quindici netti, netti;
sono vecchia diggià.

SHARPLESS

Quindici anni!

PINKERTON

Quindici anni!

SHARPLESS

L'età dei giuochi . . .

PINKERTON

. . . e dei confetti.

GORO

L'Imperial Commissario, l'Ufficiale
del registro, i congiunti.

PINKERTON

Fate presto.
Che burletta la sfilata
della nova parentela,
tolta in prestito, a mesata!

PARENTI, AMICHE

Dov'è? Dov'è?

BUTTERFLY, AMICHE

Eccolo là!

LA CUGINA, PARENTI

Bello non è, . . .

SHARPLESS

Twenty.

BUTTERFLY

Lower.
Just fifteen exactly;
I am old already.

SHARPLESS

Fifteen years old!

PINKERTON

Fifteen years old!

SHARPLESS

The age for games . . .

PINKERTON

. . . and for sweets.

GORO

The Imperial Commissioner, the official
from the registry, the relatives.

PINKERTON

Get ready, quickly.
What a farce—this procession
of my new relatives
hired by the month!

RELATIONS, FRIENDS

Where is he? Where is he?

BUTTERFLY, FRIENDS

There he is!

COUSIN, RELATIONS

He's not handsome, . . .

PINKERTON

Certo . . .
. . . dietro a quella . . .

BUTTERFLY

Bello è così . . .

AMICHE

Mi pare un re!

PINKERTON

. . . vela di ventaglio . . .

BUTTERFLY

. . . che non si può sognar di più.

PARENTI

. . . in verità. Vale un Perù.

PINKERTON

. . . pavonazzo, . . .

LA MADRE

Mi pare un re!

PARENTI

Bello non è.

PINKERTON

. . . la mia suocera si cela.

PARENTI

Vale un Perù!

AMICHE

Mi pare un re!

LA CUGINA

Goro l'offrì pur anco a me.

PINKERTON

. . . I'm sure . . .
. . . behind the . . .

BUTTERFLY

He is so handsome . . .

FRIENDS

I think he's like a king!

PINKERTON

. . . shelter of that . . .

BUTTERFLY

. . . you couldn't imagine anyone better looking.

RELATIONS

. . . to be sure! But he's worth a mint of money.

PINKERTON

. . . gaily-coloured fan, . . .

MOTHER

I think he's like a king!

RELATIONS

He's not handsome.

PINKERTON

. . . my mother-in-law is hiding.

RELATIONS

He's worth a mint of money.

FRIENDS

I think he's like a king.

COUSIN

Goro offered him to me, too.

BUTTERFLY

Sì, giusto tu!

PINKERTON

E quel coso da strappazzo . . .
. . . è lo zio briaco e pazzo.

AMICHE

Ecco, perchè prescelta fu,
vuol far con te la soprappiù!

PARENTI

La sua beltà già disfiorì.

AMICHE

Divorzierà.

LA CUGINA, PARENTI

Spero di sì.

AMICHE

Spero di sì.

PARENTI

La sua beltà già disfiorì.

GORO

Per carità tacete un po'.

YAKUSIDE

Vino ce n'è?

LA MADRE, LA ZIA

Guardiamo un po'.

PARENTI

Ne vidi già, . . .
. . . color di tè, e chermisì.

AMICHE

La sua beltà già disfiorì . . .
. . . Divorzierà.

BUTTERFLY

Indeed!

PINKERTON

And that common fellow . . .
. . . is her drunken and crazy uncle.

FRIENDS

There you are, because she was chosen,
she thinks she's better than you are.

RELATIONS

Her beauty is already fading.

FRIENDS

There'll be a divorce.

COUSIN, RELATIONS

I hope so.

FRIENDS

I hope so.

RELATIONS

Her beauty is already fading.

GORO

For goodness' sake, be a little quieter.

UNCLE YAKUSIDE

Is there any wine?

MOTHER, AUNT

Let's have a look.

RELATIONS

We've just seen some . . .
. . . tea-coloured, and some red.

FRIENDS

Her beauty is already fading . . .
. . . There'll be a divorce.

LA MADRE, LA ZIA, AMICHE,
PARENTI

Ah! hu! ah! hu! ah! hu!

LA CUGINA

Goro l'offrì . . .

LA MADRE

Mi pare un re!

PARENTI

Bello non è, . . .

AMICHE

Bello è così . . .

LA CUGINA

. . . pur anco a me, . . .

LA ZIA

Vale un Perù.

YAKUSIDE

Vino ce n'è?

PARENTI

. . . in verità, . . .

AMICHE

. . . che non si può . . .

LA CUGINA

. . . ma s'ebbe un no!

LA MADRE, LA ZIA

In verità, . . .

YAKUSIDE

Guardiamo un po', . . .

MOTHER, AUNT, FRIENDS,
RELATIONS

Ah! Ooh! Ah! Ooh!

COUSIN

Goro offered him . . .

MOTHER

I think he's like a king!

RELATIONS

He's not handsome, . . .

FRIENDS

He's so handsome . . .

COUSIN

. . . to me, too, . . .

AUNT

He's worth a fortune.

UNCLE YAKUSIDE

Is there any wine?

RELATIONS

. . . truly, . . .

FRIENDS

. . . one couldn't . . .

COUSIN

. . . but he got no for an answer!

MOTHER, AUNT

Truly, . . .

UNCLE YAKUSIDE

Let's see, . . .

PARENTI	**RELATIONS**
. . . bello non è!	. . . he's not handsome!
AMICHE	**FRIENDS**
. . . sognar di più!	. . . dream of anything more so!
BUTTERFLY	**BUTTERFLY**
Si, giusto tu!	Naturally, of course!
YAKUSIDE	**UNCLE YAKUSIDE**
. . . guardiamo . . .	. . . let's have . . .
PARENTI	**RELATIONS**
Bello, . . .	Handsome, . . .
LA CUGINA, PARENTI	**COUSIN, RELATIONS**
. . . bello non è, *etc.*	. . . he's not handsome, *etc.*
LA MADRE, LA ZIA	**MOTHER, AUNT**
. . . bello è così, *etc.*	. . . he's so handsome, *etc.*
YAKUSIDE	**UNCLE YAKUSIDE**
. . . un po', *etc.*	. . . a look, *etc.*
AMICHE	**FRIENDS**
Mi pare un re, *etc.*	He's like a king, *etc.*
GORO	**GORO**
Per carità, tacete un po'. Sch! Sch! Sch!	For goodness' sake, be a little quieter. Sh!
SHARPLESS	**SHARPLESS**
O amico fortunato!	Oh my friend, how fortunate you are!
LA CUGINA, PARENTI	**COUSIN, RELATIONS**
Ei l'offrì pur . . .	He offered him . . .
LA MADRE, AMICHE	**MOTHER, FRIENDS**
Egli è bel, mi . . .	He is handsome, . . .

PINKERTON

Si, è vero, . . .

SHARPLESS

O, . . .

LA CUGINA, PARENTI

. . . anco a me!

LA MADRE, AMICHE

. . . pare un re!

PINKERTON

. . . è un fiore, un fiore! . . .

SHARPLESS

. . . fortunato Pinkerton, . . .

LA CUGINA, PARENTI

Ei l'offrì, *etc.*, . . .

LA MADRE, AMICHE

Egli è bel, *etc.*

PINKERTON

L'esotico suo odore . . .

SHARPLESS

. . . che in sorte v'è toccato . . .

LA CUGINA, PARENTI

. . . ma risposi non lo vo'!

LA MADRE, AMICHE

Non avrei risposto no!

PINKERTON

. . . m'ha il cervello sconvolto.

PINKERTON

Yes, truly, . . .

SHARPLESS

Oh, . . .

COUSIN, RELATIONS

. . . to me, too!

MOTHER, FRIENDS

. . . I think he's like a king!

PINKERTON

. . . she's a flower . . .

SHARPLESS

. . . lucky Pinkerton, . . .

COUSIN, RELATIONS

He offered him, *etc.*, . . .

MOTHER, FRIENDS

He is handsome, *etc.*

PINKERTON

. . . whose exotic fragrance . . .

SHARPLESS

. . . to whom fate has given . . .

COUSIN, RELATIONS

. . . but I answered I don't want him.

MOTHER, FRIENDS

I shouldn't have answered no.

PINKERTON

. . . has completely turned my head.

SHARPLESS

. . . un fior pur or sbocciato!

LA CUGINA, PARENTI

E risposi: no!

LA MADRE, AMICHE

Non direi mai no!

SHARPLESS

Non più bella e d'assai . . .

LA CUGINA, PARENTI

Senza tanto ricercar . . .

LA MADRE, AMICHE

No, mie care, non mi par, . . .

BUTTERFLY

Badate, attenti a me.

PINKERTON

Sì, è vero, è un fiore, . . .

SHARPLESS

. . . fanciulla io vidi mai di questa . . .

PINKERTON

. . . e in fede . . .

SHARPLESS

. . . Butterfly, . . .

LA CUGINA, PARENTI

. . . io ne trovo dei miglior, . . .

LA MADRE, AMICHE

. . . è davvero un gran signor, . . .

SHARPLESS

. . . this flower now bursting into bloom!

COUSIN, RELATIONS

I answered no!

MOTHER, FRIENDS

I should never have said no!

SHARPLESS

A more beautiful creature . . .

COUSIN, RELATIONS

Without looking all that hard . . .

MOTHER, FRIENDS

No, my dears, I don't think so; . . .

BUTTERFLY

Here, listen to me.

PINKERTON

Yes, truly, she's a flower, . . .

SHARPLESS

. . . I've never seen . . .

PINKERTON

. . . and upon my honour, . . .

SHARPLESS

. . . Butterfly, . . .

COUSIN, RELATIONS

. . . I could have found better . . .

MOTHER, FRIENDS

. . . he's a real gentleman, . . .

PINKERTON

. . . mia l'ho colto!

SHARPLESS

. . . e se a voi sembran . . .

LA CUGINA, PARENTI

. . . e gli dirò un bel no, . . .

LA MADRE, AMICHE

. . . nè gli direi di no, . . .

UOMINI

E divorzierà, . . .

SHARPLESS

. . . scede il patto e la sua . . .

LA CUGINA, PARENTI

. . . e gli dirò di no, di no!

LA MADRE, AMICHE

. . . nè mai direi di no, di no!

UOMINI

. . . e divorzierà, divorzierà!

SHARPLESS

. . . fede, badate! Ella ci crede.

BUTTERFLY

Mamma, vien qua.
Badate a me:
attenti, orsù,
uno, due, tre
e tutti giù.

PINKERTON

. . . I've picked it!

SHARPLESS

. . . and if to you this contract . . .

COUSIN, RELATIONS

. . . and I shall tell him definitely not,

MOTHER, FRIENDS

. . . and I would not say no, . . .

SOME MEN

. . . and there'll be a divorce!

SHARPLESS

. . . a mockery, take care! She trusts
you.

COUSIN, RELATIONS

. . . and I shall tell him definitely not . . .

MOTHER, FRIENDS

. . . and I would not say no . . .

SOME MEN

. . . and there'll be a divorce!

SHARPLESS

. . . take care! She trusts you.

BUTTERFLY

Mother, come here.
Listen to me:
pay attention,
one, two, three
and everyone down.

PINKERTON

Vieni, amor mio!
Vi piace la casetta?

BUTTERFLY

Signor F. B. Pinkerton . . . perdono . . .
Io vorrei . . . pochi oggetti da donna . . .

PINKERTON

Dove sono?

BUTTERFLY

Sono qui . . . vi dispiace?

PINKERTON

O perchè mai, mia bella Butterfly?

BUTTERFLY

Fazzoletti. La pipa. Una cintura.
Un piccolo fermaglio.
Uno specchio. Un ventaglio.

PINKERTON

Quel barattolo?

BUTTERFLY

Un vaso di tintura.

PINKERTON

Ohibò!

BUTTERFLY

Vi spiace? . . .
Via!

PINKERTON

E quello?

BUTTERFLY

Cosa sacra e mia.

PINKERTON

Come, my love!
Do you like our little house?

BUTTERFLY

Mister F. B. Pinkerton . . . excuse me
I should like . . . a few feminine things

PINKERTON

Where are they?

BUTTERFLY

They're here . . . you don't mind?

PINKERTON

Why ever should I, my lovely Butterfly?

BUTTERFLY

Handkerchiefs. A pipe. A sash.
A little brooch.
A mirror. A fan.

PINKERTON

What's that pot?

BUTTERFLY

A jar of rouge.

PINKERTON

Shame on you!

BUTTERFLY

You don't like it? . . .
Away with it!

PINKERTON

And that?

BUTTERFLY

A sacred possession of mine.

PINKERTON	PINKERTON
E non si può vedere?	Can't I see it?
BUTTERFLY	BUTTERFLY
C'è troppa gente. Perdonate.	There are too many people. Forgive me.
GORO	GORO
È un presente del Mikado a suo padre . . . coll'invito . . .	It was a present from the Mikado to her father, inviting him to . . .
PINKERTON	PINKERTON
E suo padre?	And her father?
GORO	GORO
Ha obbedito.	Obeyed.
BUTTERFLY	BUTTERFLY
Gli Ottokè.	The Ottoke.
PINKERTON	PINKERTON
Quei pupazzi? Avete detto?	These dolls? What did you say they were?
BUTTERFLY	BUTTERFLY
Son l'anime degli avi.	They are the spirits of my ancestors.
PINKERTON	PINKERTON
Ah! il mio rispetto.	Oh! My respects to them.
BUTTERFLY	BUTTERFLY
Ieri son salita tutta sola in secreto alla Missione. Colla nuova mia vita posso adottare nuova religione. Lo zio Bonzo nol sa, nè i miei lo sanno. Io seguo il mio destino, e piena d'umiltà al Dio del signor Pinkerton m'inchino. È il mio destino.	Yesterday I went out all alone, and in secret, to the Mission. With my new life I want to adopt a new religion. My uncle, the Bonze, doesn't know, nor do my relations. I follow my destiny and, full of humility, bow to Mister Pinkerton's God. It is my destiny.

Nella stessa chiesetta
in ginocchio con voi
pregherò lo stesso Dio.
E per farvi contento
potrò forse obliar la gente mia.
Amore' mio!

GORO

Tutti zitti!

COMMISSIONER

È concesso al nominato
Benjamin Franklin Pinkerton
Luogotenente nella cannoniera
"Lincoln",
marina degli Stati Uniti, America del
Nord;
ed alla damigella Butterfly
del quartiere d'Omara, Nagasaki,
d'unirsi in matrimonio,
per dritto il primo, della propria
volontà,
ed ella per consenso dei parenti
qui testimonî all'atto.

GORO

Lo sposo.
Poi la sposa.
E tutto è fatto.

AMICHE

Madama Butterfly!

BUTTERFLY

Madama F. B. Pinkerton.

IL COMMISSARIO IMPERIALE

Auguri molti.

PINKERTON

I miei ringraziamenti.

In the same little church,
kneeling with you,
I will pray to the same God.
And in order to please you
perhaps I shall be able to forget my
people.
Oh my love!

GORO

Quiet, everyone!

COMMISSIONER

Permission is granted to the herein
named
Benjamin Franklin Pinkerton,
Lieutenant in the gunboat "Lincoln",
United States Navy, North America;
and to Miss Butterfly
of the Omara district of Nagasaki,
to be joined together in matrimony,
the former by his own free will,
the latter with the consent of her
relatives
who are witnesses to the contract.

GORO

The bridegroom.
Now the bride.
And it's all done.

FRIENDS

Madam Butterfly!

BUTTERFLY

Madam F. B. Pinkerton.

COMMISSIONER

My best wishes.

PINKERTON

Many thanks.

IL COMMISSARIO IMPERIALE	**COMMISSIONER**
Il signor Console scende?	Are you leaving, sir?
SHARPLESS	**SHARPLESS**
L'accompagno. Ci vedrem domani.	I'll go with him. We'll see each other tomorrow.
PINKERTON	**PINKERTON**
A meraviglia.	Marvellous.
REGISTRAR	**REGISTRAR**
Posterità.	May you have many descendants.
PINKERTON	**PINKERTON**
Mi proverò.	I'll do my best.
SHARPLESS	**SHARPLESS**
Giudizio!	Be sensible!
PINKERTON	**PINKERTON**
Ed eccoci in famiglia! Sbrighiamoci al più presto in modo onesto.	And here we are, at home together. Let's hurry and be rid of these people as soon as we can, without being impolite.
Hip! Hip!	Cheers!
AMICHE	**FRIENDS**
O Kami! o Kami!	O Kami! O Kami!
PINKERTON	**PINKERTON**
Beviamo ai novissimi legami.	Let us drink to the new bond between us.
YAKUSIDE, PARENTI	**UNCLE YAKUSIDE, RELATIONS**
O Kami! o Kami!	O Kami! O Kami!
PINKERTON	**PINKERTON**
Beviamo, *etc.*	Let us drink, *etc.*

LA MADRE, LA CUGINA	MOTHER, COUSIN
Beviamo, beviamo.	Let us drink.
LA MADRE, LA CUGINA, AMICHE	MOTHER, COUSIN, FRIENDS
O Kami! o Kami! Beviamo, *etc.*	O Kami! O Kami! Let us drink, etc.
VOCE DEL BONZO	VOICE OF THE BONZE
Ciociosan! Ciociosan! Abbominazione!	Cho-Cho-San! Cho-Cho-San! What an abomination!
BUTTERFLY, AMICHE	BUTTERFLY, FRIENDS
Lo zio Bonzo!	My } Her } uncle the Bonze!
GORO	GORO
Un corno al . . . . . . guastafeste!	Damn the . . . . . . spoil-sport!
IL BONZO	BONZE
Ciociosan!	Cho-Cho-San!
GORO	GORO
Chi ci leva d'intorno . . . . . . le persone moleste?	Who will rid us . . . . . . of such annoying creatures?
IL BONZO	BONZE
Ciociosan! . . . Ciociosan! Ciociosan! Che hai tu fatto alla Missione?	Cho-Cho-San! . . . Cho-Cho-San! Cho-Cho-San! What did you do at the Mission?
LA CUGINA, AMICHE	COUSIN, FRIENDS
Rispondi, Ciociosan!	Answer, Cho-Cho-San!
PINKERTON	PINKERTON
Che mi strilla quel matto?	What's that madman shouting about?
IL BONZO	BONZE
Rispondi, che hai tu fatto?	Answer me, what did you do?
AMICHE, PARENTI	FRIENDS, RELATIONS
Rispondi, Ciociosan!	Answer, Cho-Cho-San!

IL BONZO	BONZE
Come, hai tu gli occhi asciutti?	What, can your eyes be dry?
Son dunque questi i frutti?	Are these, then, the fruits?
Ci ha rinnegato tutti!	She renounced us all!
AMICHE, PARENTI	FRIENDS, RELATIONS
Hou! Ciociosan!	Ooh! Cho-Cho-San!
IL BONZO	BONZE
Rinnegato, vi dico, il culto antico.	Renounced, I tell you, the ancient cult.
AMICHE, PARENTI	FRIENDS, RELATIONS
Hou! Ciociosan!	Ooh! Cho-Cho-San!
IL BONZO	BONZE
Kami sarundasico!	Kami sarundasico!
AMICHE, PARENTI	FRIENDS, RELATIONS
Hou! Ciociosan!	Ooh! Cho-Cho-San!
IL BONZO	BONZE
All'anima tua guasta	What torments threaten
qual supplizio sovrasta!	your lost soul!
PINKERTON	PINKERTON
Ehi, dico: basta, basta!	Hey, you: that's enough, I say!
IL BONZO	BONZE
Venite tutti! Andiamo!	Come, everyone! Let's go!
Ci hai rinnegato e noi ...	You have renounced us and we ...
IL BONZO, PARENTI, AMICHE	BONZE, RELATIONS, FRIENDS
... ti rinneghiamo!	... renounce you!
PINKERTON	PINKERTON
Sbarazzate all'istante. In casa mia	Get out of here this instant. In my house
niente baccano e niente bonzeria.	there'll be no uproar and no "bonzery".
AMICHE, PARENTI	FRIENDS, RELATIONS
Hou!	Ooh!

Hou! Ciociosan! Hou! Ciociosan!

Ooh! Cho-Cho-San! Ooh! Cho-Cho-San!

IL BONZO, PARENTI, AMICHE

Kami sarundasico!
Hou! Ciociosan!
Ti rinneghiamo!
Hou! Ciociosan!
Hou! Ciociosan!

BONZE, RELATIONS, FRIENDS

Kami sarundasico!
Ooh! Cho-Cho-San!
We renounce you!
Ooh! Cho-Cho-San!
Ooh! Cho-Cho-San!

PINKERTON

Bimba, bimba, non piangere per
gracchiar . . .
. . . di ranocchi.

PINKERTON

Sweet child, do not weep because of the
croaking . . .
. . . of these frogs.

AMICHE, PARENTI

Hou! Ciociosan!

FRIENDS, RELATIONS

Ooh! Cho-Cho-San!

BUTTERFLY

Urlano ancor!

BUTTERFLY

They're still crying out!

PINKERTON

Tutta la tua tribù
e i Bonzi tutti del Giappon
non valgono il pianto di quegli
occhi cari e belli.

PINKERTON

All your tribe
and all the Bonzes in Japan
are not worth a tear from those
dear, lovely eyes.

BUTTERFLY

Davver?
Non piango più.
E quasi del ripudio non mi duole
per le vostre parole
che mi suonan così dolci nel cor.

BUTTERFLY

Do you mean that?
I shan't cry any more.
And I hardly mind their repudiation,
for your words
sound so sweet to my heart.

PINKERTON

Che fai? La man?

PINKERTON

What are you doing? My hand?

BUTTERFLY

M'han detto
che laggiù fra la gente costumata
è questo il segno del maggior rispetto.

BUTTERFLY

I was told
that over there, among well-mannered
people,
it's a sign of the highest respect.

SUZUKI

E Izaghi ed Izanami sarundasico,
e Kami, e Izaghi ed Izanami,
sarundasico, e Kami.

PINKERTON

Chi brontola lassù?

BUTTERFLY

È Suzuki che fa la sua preghiera seral.

PINKERTON

Viene la sera . . .

BUTTERFLY

. . . e l'ombra e la quiete.

PINKERTON

E sei qui sola.

BUTTERFLY

Sola e rinnegata!
Rinnegata e felice!

PINKERTON

A voi, chiudete.

BUTTERFLY

Sì, sì, noi tutti soli.
E fuori il mondo.

PINKERTON

E il Bonzo furibondo.

BUTTERFLY

Suzuki, le mie vesti.

SUZUKI

Buona notte.

SUZUKI

And Izaghi and Izanami sarundasico
and Kami, and Izaghi and Izanami,
sarundasico, and Kami.

PINKERTON

Who's muttering in there?

BUTTERFLY

It's Suzuki saying her evening prayers.

PINKERTON

Night is falling . . .

BUTTERFLY

. . . and darkness and peace.

PINKERTON

And you are here alone.

BUTTERFLY

Alone and renounced!
Renounced and happy!

PINKERTON

You, close up.

BUTTERFLY

Yes, yes, we are all alone.
And outside is the world.

PINKERTON

And the raging Bonze.

BUTTERFLY

Suzuki, my clothes.

SUZUKI

Good night.

BUTTERFLY

Quest'obi pomposa di scioglier mi
tarda . . .
. . . si vesta la sposa . . .

PINKERTON

Con moti di scoiattolo
i nodi allenta e scioglie!

BUTTERFLY

. . . di puro candor.

PINKERTON

Pensar che quel giocattolo
è mia moglie!

BUTTERFLY

Tra motti sommessi sorride . . .

PINKERTON

Mia moglie!

BUTTERFLY

. . . e mi guarda. Celarmi potessi!

PINKERTON

Ma tal grazia dispiega, . . .

BUTTERFLY

Ne ho tanto rossor!

PINKERTON

. . . ch'io mi struggo per la . . .

BUTTERFLY

E ancor l'irata voce . . .

PINKERTON

. . . febbre d'un subito desio!

BUTTERFLY

I long to be rid of this showy
sash . . .
. . . The bride now dresses . . .

PINKERTON

Her movements are delicate as a
squirrel's
as she loosens the knots!

BUTTERFLY

. . . in spotless white.

PINKERTON

To think that this little plaything
is my wife!

BUTTERFLY

Talking quietly, he smiles . . .

PINKERTON

My wife!

BUTTERFLY

. . . and watches me. If only I could
hide!

PINKERTON

But she displays such grace . . .

BUTTERFLY

He makes me blush so!

PINKERTON

. . . that I'm consumed by a sudden . . .

BUTTERFLY

And still the angry voice . . .

PINKERTON

. . . fever of desire!

BUTTERFLY

. . . mi maledice.
Butterfly rinnegata . . .
rinnegata e felice.

PINKERTON

Bimba dagli occhi pieni di malìa
ora sei tutta mia.
Sei tutta vestita di giglio.
Mi piace la treccia tua bruna
fra candidi veli.

BUTTERFLY

Somiglio la dea della luna,
la piccola dea della luna,
che scende la notte
dal ponte del ciel . . .

PINKERTON

. . . e affascina i cuori.

BUTTERFLY

E li prende, e li avvolge
in un bianco mantel
e via se li reca
negli alti reami.

PINKERTON

Ma intanto finor non m'hai detto,
ancor non m'hai detto che m'ami.
Le sa quella dea le parole
che appagan gli ardenti desir?

BUTTERFLY

Le sa.
Forse dirle non vuole
per tema d'averne a morir.

PINKERTON

Stolta paura, l'amor non uccide
ma dà vita, e sorride
per gioie celestiali

BUTTERFLY

. . . is cursing me.
Butterfly, renounced . . .
renounced and happy.

PINKERTON

Sweet child with the bewitching eyes,
now you are all mine.
You are dressed like a lily.
I like your brown tresses
amidst your white veils.

BUTTERFLY

I am like the goddess of the moon,
the little goddess of the moon,
who descends at night
from the bridge of the sky . . .

PINKERTON

. . . and bewitches all hearts.

BUTTERFLY

And takes them and wraps them
in a white cloak
and carries them away
to the realms above.

PINKERTON

But you haven't yet told me,
you haven't yet told me you love me.
Does this goddess know the words
that gratify ardent desire?

BUTTERFLY

She does.
Perhaps she doesn't want to say them
for fear of dying at hearing them.

PINKERTON

Foolish fear—love doesn't kill
but gives life, and smiles
with heavenly joy,

come ora fa
nei tuoi lunghi occhi ovali.

BUTTERFLY

Adesso voi siete per me
l'occhio del firmamento.
E mi piaceste dal primo momento
che vi ho veduto.
Siete alto, forte.
Ridete con modi sì palesi!
E dite cose che mai non intesi.
Or son contenta, or son contenta.
Vogliatemi bene,
un bene piccolino.
un bene da bambino
quale a me si conviene.
Vogliatemi bene.
Noi siamo gente avvezza
alle piccole cose
umili e silenziose,
ad una tenerezza
sfiorante e pur profonda
come il ciel, come l'onda
del mare.

PINKERTON

Dammi ch'io baci le tue mani care . . .
Mia Butterfly! come t'han ben nomata
tenue farfalla.

BUTTERFLY

Dicon ch'oltre mare
se cade in man dell'uom,
ogni farfalla da uno
spillo è trafitta
ed in tavola infitta!

PINKERTON

Un po' di vero c'è
E tu lo sai perchè?
Perchè non fugga più.
Io t'ho ghermita.
Ti serro palpitante.
Sei mia.

BUTTERFLY

For me you are now
the centre of the universe.
I liked you from the first moment
I saw you.
You are tall and strong.
You laugh so frankly!
And you say things I've never heard
before.
Now I am happy, I am happy!
Love me,
just a little,
a child-like love
to suit a child like me.
Love me!
We are a race accustomed
to little things,
humble and quiet
to a tenderness gently
caressing, yet as profound
as the sky and the rolling sea.

PINKERTON

Let me kiss your dear hands . . . My
Butterfly! How aptly you were named
slender butterfly!

BUTTERFLY

They say that, in other lands,
if a butterfly
falls into a man's hands,
she is transfixed with a pin
and fastened to a board!

PINKERTON

There's some truth in that.
And do you know why?
So that she won't fly away.
I've caught you.
I press you to me as you tremble.
You are mine.

BUTTERFLY

Sì, per la vita.

PINKERTON

Vieni, vieni.
Via dall'anima in pena
l'angoscia paurosa!
È notte serena!
Guarda: dorme ogni cosa!

BUTTERFLY

Ah! dolce notte!

PINKERTON

Vieni, vieni.

BUTTERFLY

Quante stelle! Non . . .
. . . le vidi mai sì belle!

PINKERTON

È notte serena! . . .
. . . Ah! vieni, vieni; è notte serena!

Guarda: dorme ogni cosa!

BUTTERFLY

Dolce notte! Quante stelle!

PINKERTON

Vieni, vieni!

BUTTERFLY

Non le vidi mai sì belle!

PINKERTON

Vieni, vieni!

BUTTERFLY

Trema, brilla ogni favilla . . .

BUTTERFLY

Yes, for life.

PINKERTON

Come, oh come.
Banish from your troubled heart
all pangs of fear!
The night is peaceful!
See, everything is sleeping!

BUTTERFLY

Ah! Sweet night!

PINKERTON

Come, oh come.

BUTTERFLY

So many stars! Never . . .
. . . have I seen them so beautiful!

PINKERTON

The night is peaceful! . . .
. . . Come, oh come; the night is
peaceful!
See, everything is sleeping!

BUTTERFLY

Sweet night! So many stars!

PINKERTON

Come, oh come!

BUTTERFLY

Never have I seen them so beautiful!

PINKERTON

Come, oh come!

BUTTERFLY

Each little spark trembles, and shines, . . .

PINKERTON

Vien, sei mia!

BUTTERFLY

. . . col baglior d'una pupilla.

PINKERTON

Via l'angoscia dal tuo cor!

BUTTERFLY

Oh! . . .
. . . Oh! . . .
. . . quanti occhi fissi, attenti, . . .

PINKERTON

Ti serro palpitante, . . .
. . . sei mia!

BUTTERFLY

. . . d'ogni parte a riguardar! . . .

PINKERTON

Ah! vien, vien, sei mia!

BUTTERFLY

. . . pei firmamente, via pei lidi, via pel mare!

PINKERTON

Vieni, guarda: dorme ogni cosa! . . .
. . . Ti serro palpitante.
Ah, vien!

BUTTERFLY

Ah! quanti occhi fissi, attenti! Quanti sguardi!

PINKERTON

Guarda: dorme ogni cosa. Ah, vien!

PINKERTON

Come, you are mine!

BUTTERFLY

. . . with the brightness of an eye.

PINKERTON

Banish all fear from your heart!

BUTTERFLY

Oh! . . .
. . . Oh! . . .
. . . all those eyes fixed and watching . . .

PINKERTON

I press you to me as you tremble . . .
. . . you are mine!

BUTTERFLY

. . . looking from all sides, . . .

PINKERTON

Oh, come, come, you are mine!

BUTTERFLY

. . . from the sky, along the shore, and over the sea!

PINKERTON

Come, see, everything is sleeping! . . .
. . . I press you to me as you tremble.
Oh, come!

BUTTERFLY

Ah! So many eyes fixed and watching all looking, looking!

PINKERTON

See, everything is sleeping. Oh come!

BUTTERFLY

Ride il ciel!

PINKERTON

Ah! vieni, vieni!

BUTTERFLY

Ah! dolce . . .
. . . notte! Tutto estatico d'amor ride il
ciel!

PINKERTON

Ah! vien! ah! vien! sei mia!

BUTTERFLY

The sky is smiling!

PINKERTON

Come, oh come!

BUTTERFLY

Ah! Sweet . . .
. . . night! Filled with the ecstasy of
love, the sky is smiling!

PINKERTON

Come, oh come! You are mine!

ATTO SECONDO

PARTE PRIMA

Interno della casetta di Butterfly.

SUZUKI

E Izaghi ed Izanami,
Sarundasico e Kami.
Oh! la mia testa!
E tu Ten-Sjoo-daj!
fate che Butterfly
non pianga più, mai più.

BUTTERFLY

Pigri ed obesi
son gli dei giapponesi.
L'americano Iddio, sono persuasa,
ben più presto risponde
a chi l'implori.
Ma temo ch'egli ignori
che noi siam qui di casa.
Suzuki, è lungi la miseria?

SUZUKI

Questo è l'ultimo fondo.

BUTTERFLY

Questo? Oh! Troppe spese!

SUZUKI

S'egli non torna e presto,
siamo male in arnese.

BUTTERFLY

Ma torna.

SUZUKI

Tornerà!

ACT II

PART I

Inside Butterfly's house.

SUZUKI

And Izaghi and Izanami,
Sarundasico and Kami.
Oh my head!
And thou, Ten-Sjoo-daj,
May Butterfly
weep no more, no more.

BUTTERFLY

Fat and lazy
are the Japanese gods.
The American God, I'm certain,
answers more promptly
those who pray to him.
But I fear he doesn't know
we're living here.
Suzuki, how long before we run out of
money?

SUZUKI

This is all there is left.

BUTTERFLY

This? Oh! We've spent too much!

SUZUKI

If he doesn't return, and quickly,
we shall be in a bad way.

BUTTERFLY

But he's coming back.

SUZUKI

He will come back!

BUTTERFLY

Perchè dispone che il Console
provveda alla pigione, rispondi, su!
Perchè con tante cure
la casa rifornì di serrature,
s'ei non volesse ritornar mai più?

SUZUKI

Non lo so.

BUTTERFLY

Non lo sai?
Io te lo dico: per tener ben fuori
le zanzare, i parenti ed i dolori,
e dentro, con gelosa
custodia, la sua sposa,
la sua sposa che son io—Butterfly!

SUZUKI

Mai non s'è udito
di straniero marito
che sia tornato al suo nido.

BUTTERFLY

Ah! taci, o t'uccido.
Quell ultima mattina:
"Tornerete, signor?" gli domandai.
Egli, col cuore grosso,
per celarmi la pena, sorridendo rispose:
"O Butterfly, piccina mogliettina,
tornerò colle rose
alla stagion serena
quando fa la nidiata il pettirosso."
Tornerà.

SUZUKI

Speriam.

BUTTERFLY

Dillo con me: Tornerà.

SUZUKI

Tornerà.

BUTTERFLY

Why did he arrange for the Consul
to see to the rent? Answer that!
Why with such care
did he fit the house with locks,
if he intended never to return again?

SUZUKI

I don't know.

BUTTERFLY

You don't know?
I'll tell you: to keep mosquitoes,
relatives and troubles outside,
and inside, jealously guarded,
his bride—
His bride—me—Butterfly!

SUZUKI

But it's unknown for a foreign
husband to come back
to his home.

BUTTERFLY

Ah, be quiet, or I'll kill you!
That last morning I asked him:
'Will you come back, my lord?'
He, with heavy heart, trying to hide
his sorrow from me, answered with a
smile:
'Oh Butterfly, my darling little wife,
I shall return with the roses,
in that happy season
when the robin makes his nest.'
He will return.

SUZUKI

Let us hope so.

BUTTERFLY

Say it with me: He will return.

SUZUKI

He will return.

BUTTERFLY

Piangi? Perchè? Perchè?
Ah, la fede ti manca!
Senti.

Un bel dì, vedremo
levarsi un fil di fumo
sull'estremo
confin del mare,
e poi la nave appare.
Poi la nave bianca
entra nel porto,
romba il suo saluto—
vedi? Egli è venuto!
Io non gli scendo incontro.
Io no. Mi metto
là sul ciglio del colle e aspetto,
e aspetto gran tempo e non mi pesa
la lunga attesa.
E uscito dalla folla cittadina
un uomo, un picciol punto,
s'avvia per la collina.
Chi sarà? chi sarà?
E come sarà giunto
che dirà? che dirà?
Chiamerà Butterfly dalla lontana.
Io, senza dar risposta,
me ne starò nascosta
un po' per celia, e un po'
per non morir
al primo incontro,
ed egli alquanto in pena
chiamerà, chiamerà,
'Piccina mogliettina
olezzo di verbena,'
i nomi che mi dava al suo venire.
Tutto questo avverrà,
te lo prometto.
Tienti la tua paura,
io con sicura fede l'aspetto.

BUTTERFLY

You weep? Why?
Oh, you have no faith!
Listen.

One fine day, we shall see
a wisp of smoke rising
over the farthest
horizon of the sea,
and then the ship will appear.
Then the white ship
enters the harbour,
thundering out its salute—
you see? He has come!
I don't go down to meet him.
Not I. I stand
on the brow of the hill and wait,
and wait a long time and do not weary
of the long waiting.
And out of the crowded city there
comes
a man—a tiny speck—
who makes his way up the hill.
Who can it be? Who can it be?
And when he arrives,
what will he say? What will he say?
He'll call Butterfly from the distance.
I, without answering,
will stay hidden
partly for fun, and partly
so as not to die
at our first meeting.
And he, a little troubled,
will call, will call:
'My little wife,
my sweet-scented flower,'
the names he used to call me when he
came.
All this will happen,
I promise you.
Dispel your fears:
I, with unshakable faith, will await him.

GORO

C'è. Entrate.

GORO

She's there. Go in.

SHARPLESS

Chiedo scusa . . . Madama Butterfly . . .

SHARPLESS

Excuse me . . . Madam Butterfly . . .

BUTTERFLY

Madama Pinkerton, prego.
Oh!
Il mio Signor Console, Signor Console!

BUTTERFLY

Madam Pinkerton, please.
Oh!
My Consul, Mr. Consul!

SHARPLESS

Mi ravvisate?

SHARPLESS

Do you remember me?

BUTTERFLY

Benvenuto in casa americana.

BUTTERFLY

Welcome to an American home.

SHARPLESS

Grazie.

SHARPLESS

Thank you.

BUTTERFLY

Avi, antenati tutti bene?

BUTTERFLY

Your grandparents and ancestors are all
well?

SHARPLESS

Ma spero.

SHARPLESS

I hope so.

BUTTERFLY

Fumate?

BUTTERFLY

Will you smoke?

SHARPLESS

Grazie.
Ho qui . . .

SHARPLESS

Thank you.
I have here . . .

BUTTERFLY

Signore, io vedo il cielo azzurro.

BUTTERFLY

Sir, I see the sky is blue.

SHARPLESS

Grazie, no. Ho . . .

SHARPLESS

Thank you, no. I have . . .

BUTTERFLY

Preferite forse le sigarette americaine?

BUTTERFLY

Perhaps you would prefer American
cigarettes?

SHARPLESS

Grazie. Ho da mostrarvi . . .

BUTTERFLY

A voi.

SHARPLESS

Mi scrisse Benjamin Franklin Pinkerton
. . .

BUTTERFLY

Davvero! È in salute?

SHARPLESS

Perfetta.

BUTTERFLY

Io son la donna più lieta del Giappone.
Potrei farvi una domanda?

SHARPLESS

Certo.

BUTTERFLY

Quando fanno il lor nido in America
i pettirossi?

SHARPLESS

Come dite?

BUTTERFLY

Si, prima o dopo di qui?

SHARPLESS

Ma perchè?

BUTTERFLY

Mio marito m'ha promesso
di ritornar nella stagion beata
che il pettirosso rifà la nidiata.

SHARPLESS

Thank you. I have to show you . . .

BUTTERFLY

There.

SHARPLESS

Benjamin Franklin Pinkerton has
written to me . . .

BUTTERFLY

Really? Is he well?

SHARPLESS

Perfectly.

BUTTERFLY

I am the happiest woman in Japan.
May I ask you a question?

SHARPLESS

Certainly.

BUTTERFLY

When do robins make their nests in
America?

SHARPLESS

I beg your pardon?

BUTTERFLY

Yes, before or after they do here?

SHARPLESS

But why?

BUTTERFLY

My husband promised
to return in that happy season
when the robin builds its nest again.

Qui l'ha rifatta per ben tre volte,
ma può darsi che di là
usi nidiar men spesso.
Chi ride?
Oh, c'è il nakodo.
Un uom cattivo.

GORO

Godo . . .

BUTTERFLY

Zitto.
Egli osò . . . No, prima rispondete
alla dimanda mia.

SHARPLESS

Mi rincresce, ma ignoro,
non ho studiato ornitologia.

BUTTERFLY

Orni . . .

SHARPLESS

. . . tologia.

BUTTERFLY

Non lo sapete insomma.

SHARPLESS

No. Dicevamo . . .

BUTTERFLY

Ah, sì. Goro,
appena F. B. Pinkerton fu in mare,
mi venne ad assediare
con ciarle e con presenti
per ridarmi ora questo,
or quel marito.
Or promette tesori
per uno scimunito.

Here, it has done so three times already,
but perhaps over there
it nests less frequently.
Who's laughing?
Oh, it's the marriage broker.
A wicked man.

GORO

I am enjoying . . .

BUTTERFLY

Quiet.
He dared . . . No, first answer my
question.

SHARPLESS

I'm sorry, but I don't know.
I've never studied ornithology.

BUTTERFLY

Orni . . .

SHARPLESS

. . . thology.

BUTTERFLY

In fact, you don't know.

SHARPLESS

No. We were saying . . .

BUTTERFLY

Ah, yes. Goro,
as soon as F. B. Pinkerton had sailed
away,
came annoying me
with chatter and presents,
trying to make me accept first one and
then another husband.
Now he's promising great wealth
if I marry a simpleton.

GORO

Il ricco Yamadori.
Ella è povera in canna.
I suoi parenti
l'han tutti rinnegata.

BUTTERFLY

Eccolo. Attenti.
Yamadori, ancor le pene
dell'amor non v'han deluso?
Vi tagliate ancor le vene
se il mio bacio vi ricuso?

YAMADORI

Tra le cose più moleste
e l'inutil sospirar.

BUTTERFLY

Tante mogli omai toglieste.
Vi doveste abituar.

YAMADORI

L'ho sposate tutte quante
e il divorzio mi francò.

BUTTERFLY

Obbligata.

YAMADORI

A voi però . . .
. . . giurerei fede costante.

SHARPLESS

Il messaggio, ho gran paura, . . .
. . . a trasmetter non riesco.

GORO

Ville, servi, oro, ad Omara
un palazzo principesco.

GORO

The rich Yamadori.
She's as poor as can be.
All her relations
have renounced her.

BUTTERFLY

There he is. Look.
Yamadori, are you still not
disillusioned by the pangs of love?
Will you still cut your veins
if I refuse to kiss you?

YAMADORI

There are few things more trying
than hopeless sighing.

BUTTERFLY

You've had so many wives.
You ought to be used to it.

YAMADORI

I married them all,
and have been freed by divorce.

BUTTERFLY

I am flattered.

YAMADORI

But to you . . .
. . . I would swear constancy.

SHARPLESS

I'm very much afraid I shan't be able
. . . to deliver my message.

GORO

Villas, servants, gold, at Omara
a princely palace.

128

BUTTERFLY

Già legata è la mia fede.

GORO, YAMADORI

Maritata ancor si crede.

BUTTERFLY

Non mi credo: sono, sono.

GORO

Ma la legge . . .

BUTTERFLY

Io non la so.

GORO

. . . per la moglie, l'abbandono
al divorzio equiparò.

BUTTERFLY

La legge giapponese . . .
non già del mio paese.

GORO

Quale?

BUTTERFLY

Gli Stati Uniti.

SHARPLESS

Oh, l'infelice!

BUTTERFLY

Si sa che aprir la porta
e la moglie cacciar
per la più corta
qui divorziar si dice.
Ma in America questo non si può.
Vero?

SHARPLESS

Vero. Però . . .

BUTTERFLY

My troth is already plighted.

GORO, YAMADORI

She thinks she's still married.

BUTTERFLY

I don't think so, I am.

GORO

But the law . . .

BUTTERFLY

I don't know it.

GORO

. . . for the wife, has made
desertion equivalent to divorce.

BUTTERFLY

The Japanese law . . .
but not of my country.

GORO

What country?

BUTTERFLY

The United States.

SHARPLESS

Oh, the unhappy girl!

BUTTERFLY

We know that to open the door
and just chase the wife out
as quickly as possible
is called divorce here.
But in America you can't do that.
Is that not so?

SHARPLESS

That is so. However . . .

BUTTERFLY

Là, un bravo giudice
serio, impettito
dice al marito:
'Lei vuol andarsene?
Sentiam, perchè?'
'Sono seccato
del coniugato!'
E il magistrato:
'Ah, mascalzone,
presto in prigione!'
Suzuki, il tè.

GORO

Udiste?

SHARPLESS

Mi rattrista una sì piena cecità.

GORO

Segnalata è già la nave di Pinkerton.

YAMADORI

Quand'essa lo riveda . . .

SHARPLESS

Egli non vuol mostrarsi. Io venni
appunto per levarla d'inganno.

BUTTERFLY

Vostra Grazia permette . . .
Che persone moleste!

YAMADORI

Addio. Vi lascio il cuor pien
di cordoglio, ma spero ancor.

BUTTERFLY

Padrone.

BUTTERFLY

There, an honest judge,
grave and upright,
says to the husband:
'So you want to go away?
May we know why?'
'I'm bored
with married life!'
And the magistrate:
'Ah, you rascal,
into prison this instant!'
Suzuki, tea.

GORO

Do you hear?

SHARPLESS

It makes me very sad to see such
absolute blindness.

GORO

Pinkerton's ship has already been
sighted.

YAMADORI

When she sees him again . . .

SHARPLESS

He doesn't want to show himself. I
came here expressly to disillusion her.

BUTTERFLY

If your Grace will permit . . .
What tiresome people!

YAMADORI

Farewell. I leave you with my heart
full of sorrow, but still I hope.

BUTTERFLY

Just as you please.

YAMADORI

Ah! se voleste . . .

BUTTERFLY

Il guaio è che non voglio.

SHARPLESS

Ora a noi. Sedete qui.
Legger con me volete
questa lettera?

BUTTERFLY

Date.
Sulla bocca,
sul cuore.
Siete l'uomo migliore
del mondo.
Incominciate.

SHARPLESS

'Amico, cercherete
quel bel fior di fanciulla . . .'

BUTTERFLY

Dice proprio così?

SHARPLESS

Sì, così dice,
ma se ad ogni momento . . .

BUTTERFLY

Taccio, taccio, più nulla.

SHARPLESS

'Da quel tempo felice,
tre anni son passati . . .'

BUTTERFLY

Anche lui li ha contati!

YAMADORI

Ah! If only you would . . .

BUTTERFLY

The trouble is that I won't.

SHARPLESS

Now it's our turn. Sit down here.
Will you read
this letter with me?

BUTTERFLY

Give it to me.
To my lips,
on my heart.
You are the finest man
in the world.
Begin.

SHARPLESS

'My friend, seek out
that lovely flower of a girl . . .'

BUTTERFLY

Does he really say that?

SHARPLESS

Yes, that's what he says,
but if at every moment . . .

BUTTERFLY

I'll be quiet—I won't interrupt again.

SHARPLESS

'Since that happy time,
three years have passed . . .'

BUTTERFLY

He has counted them too!

SHARPLESS

'. . . e forse Butterfly
non mi rammenta più.'

BUTTERFLY

Non lo rammento?
Suzuki, dillo tu.
'Non mi rammenta più!'

SHARPLESS

Pazienza!
'Se mi vuol bene ancor,
se m'aspetta . . .'

BUTTERFLY

Oh, le dolci parole!
Tu, benedetta!

SHARPLESS

'. . . a voi mi raccomando
perchè vogliate
con circospezione prepararla . . .'

BUTTERFLY

Ritorna.

SHARPLESS

'. . . al colpo.'

BUTTERFLY

Quando? Presto! Presto!

SHARPLESS

Benone.
Qui troncarla conviene . . .
Quel diavolo d'un Pinkerton!

Ebbene, che fareste, Madama Butterfly
s'ei non dovesse ritornar più mai?

SHARPLESS

'. . . and Butterfly, perhaps,
does not remember me any more.'

BUTTERFLY

I don't remember him?
Suzuki, you tell him.
'Does not remember me any more!'

SHARPLESS

Give me patience!
'If she still loves me,
if she awaits me . . .'

BUTTERFLY

Oh, such sweet words!
You blessed letter!

SHARPLESS

'. . . I place myself in your hands
so that you may carefully
and considerately prepare her . . .'

BUTTERFLY

He's coming.

SHARPLESS

'. . . for the blow.'

BUTTERFLY

When? Quickly! Quickly!

SHARPLESS

Fine!
I must break it to her without further
ado . . .
That devil Pinkerton!
And what would you do, Madam
Butterfly,
if he were never to return again?

BUTTERFLY

Due cose potrei far:
tornar a divertir
la gente col cantar;
oppur, meglio, morire.

SHARPLESS

Di strapparvi assai mi costa
dai miraggi ingannatori.
Accogliete la proposta
di quel ricco Yamadori.

BUTTERFLY

Voi, voi signor, mi dite questo!
Voi?

SHARPLESS

Santo Dio, come si fa?

BUTTERFLY

Qui, Suzuki, presto, presto,
che Sua Grazia se ne va.

SHARPLESS

Mi scacciate?

BUTTERFLY

Ve ne prego,
già l'insistere non vale.

SHARPLESS

Fui brutale,
non lo nego.

BUTTERFLY

Oh, mi fate tanto male,
tanto male, tanto, tanto!
Niente, niente!
Ho creduto morir,
ma passa presto
come passan le nuvole sul mare.
Ah! m'ha scordata?

BUTTERFLY

I might do two things:
go back to entertaining
people with songs,
or, better, die.

SHARPLESS

It grieves me thus to rob
you of your illusions.
Accept the proposal
of the rich Yamadori.

BUTTERFLY

You, you, sir, tell me this!
You?

SHARPLESS

Oh God, what can I do?

BUTTERFLY

Here, Suzuki, quickly, quickly,
his Grace is leaving.

SHARPLESS

You're turning me out?

BUTTERFLY

Please,
forget it.

SHARPLESS

I was brutal,
I don't deny it.

BUTTERFLY

Oh, you hurt me so much,
so very, very much!
It's nothing, nothing.
I thought I was going to die,
but it soon passes,
like clouds over the sea.
Ah! Has he forgotten me?

E questo? E questo?
E questo egli potrà pure scordare?

SHARPLESS

Egli è suo?

BUTTERFLY

Chi vide mai
a bimbo del Giappon
occhi azzurrini?
E il labbro?
E i ricciolini
d'oro schietto?

SHARPLESS

È palese.
E Pinkerton lo sa?

BUTTERFLY

No. No. È nato quand'egli stava
in quel suo gran paese.
Ma voi gli scriverete che l'aspetta
un figlio senza pari!
E mi saprete dir s'ei non s'affretta ·
per le terre e pei mari!

Sai cos'ebbe cuore
di pensare quel signore?
Che tua madre dovrà
prenderti in braccio
ed alla pioggia e al vento
andar per la città
a guadagnarti il pane
e il vestimento.
Ed alle impietosite genti
la man tremante stenderà,
gridando: Udite, udite
la triste mia canzon.
A un infelice madre la carità,
muovetevi a pietà!
E Butterfly, orrible destino,
danzerà per te!
E come fece già,
la Ghesha canterà!

And this? And this?
Can he forget this as well?

SHARPLESS

Is it his?

BUTTERFLY

Whoever saw
a Japanese baby
with blue eyes?
And his mouth?
And his curls
of pure gold?

SHARPLESS

It's obvious.
And does Pinkerton know?

BUTTERFLY

No. No. The child was born when he
was away in his big country.
But you will write and tell him
that a son without equal awaits him.
And then we shall see if he doesn't
hasten over land and sea!

Do you know what that gentleman
dared to think?
That your mother will have
to take you in her arms,
and in wind and rain
go through the town
to earn money for bread
and clothing,
and to the pitying crowd
stretch out her trembling hand,
crying: Listen, listen
to my sad song.
Charity for an unhappy mother,
have pity!
And Butterfly—horrible fate—
will dance for you!
And as she used to do,
the Geisha will sing!

E la canzon giuliva e lieta
in un singhiozzo finirà!
Ah! no, no! questo mai!
Questo mestier che al disonore porta!
Morta! morta!
Mai più danzar!
Piuttosto la mia vita vo' troncar!
Ah! morta!

SHARPLESS

Quanta pietà!
Io scendo al piano. Mi perdonate?

BUTTERFLY

A te, dagli la mano.

SHARPLESS

I bei capelli biondi!
Caro, come ti chiamano?

BUTTERFLY

Rispondi:
Oggi il mio nome è Dolore.
Però dite al babbo, scrivendogli,
che il giorno del suo ritorno
Gioia, Gioia mi chiamerò.

SHARPLESS

Tuo padre lo saprà, to lo prometto.

SUZUKI

Vespa! Rospo maledetto!

BUTTERFLY

Che fu?

SUZUKI

Ci ronza intorno
il vampiro!
E ogni giorno
ai quattro venti
spargendo va

And the joyous and happy song
will end in a sob!
Ah! No, no! Never that!
That way of life which leads to dishonour!
Death! Death!
I shall never dance again!
I would rather cut short my life!
Oh! Death!

SHARPLESS

Oh, how pitiful!
I'll go now. Will you excuse me?

BUTTERFLY

There, give him your hand.

SHARPLESS

Those lovely golden curls.
Child, what is your name?

BUTTERFLY

Answer:
Today my name is Sorrow.
However, write and tell Daddy
that, the day he returns,
Joy, Joy will be my name.

SHARPLESS

Your father shall know, I promise you.

SUZUKI

Wasp! Accursed toad!

BUTTERFLY

What is it?

SUZUKI

He's whining around,
the vampire!
And every day
to the four winds
he spreads the rumour

che niuno sa
chi padre al bimbo sia!

GORO

Dicevo solo
che là in America
quando un figliolo
è nato maledetto
trarrà sempre reietto
la vita fra le genti!

BUTTERFLY

Ah! tu menti! menti! menti!
Ah! menti!
Dillo ancora e t'uccido!

SUZUKI

No!

BUTTERFLY

Va via!
Vedrai, piccolo amor,
mia pena e mio conforto,
mio piccolo amor, ah, vedrai
che il tuo vendicator
ci porterà lontano, lontan,
nella sua terra, lontan ci porterà.

SUZUKI

Il cannone del porto!
Una nave da guerra . . .

BUTTERFLY

Bianca, bianca . . . il vessillo
americano delle stelle.
Or governa per ancorare.
Reggimi la mano
ch'io ne discerna il nome,
il nome, il nome.
Eccolo: Abramo Lincoln!
Tutti han mentito! tutti! tutti!

that no one knows
who the child's father is!

GORO

I only said
that in America
when a child
is born in such circumstances
he will live forever outcast
among people!

BUTTERFLY

Ah! You lie! You lie! You lie!
Ah! You lie!
Say that again and I'll kill you!

SUZUKI

No!

BUTTERFLY

Get out!
You'll see, my little darling,
my sorrow and my comfort,
my little darling, oh, you'll see,
your avenger will take us far,
far away, to his country,
he'll take us far away.

SUZUKI

The harbour cannon!
A warship . . .

BUTTERFLY

It's white, white . . . the American
flag with the stars.
Now it's about to drop anchor.
Keep my hand steady
so that I can make out the name,
the name, the name.
There it is: Abraham Lincoln!
They were all lying! All of them! All!

Sol io lo sapevo . . .
io sol che l'amo.

Vedi lo scimunito tuo dubbio?
È giunto! È giunto! È giunto!
Proprio nel punto
che ognun diceva:
piangi e dispera,
trionfa il mio amor!
Il mio amor, la mia fè
trionfa intera.
Ei torna e m'ama!

Scuoti quella fronda
di ciliegio e m'inonda
di fior.
Io vo' tuffar
nella pioggia odorosa
l'arsa fronte.

SUZUKI

Signora,
quetatevi . . . quel pianto . . .

BUTTERFLY

No, rido, rido! Quanto
lo dovremo aspettar?
Che pensi? Un'ora?

SUZUKI

Di più.

BUTTERFLY

Due ore, forse.
Tutto, tutto sia pien di fior,
come la notte è di faville.

Va pei fior!

SUZUKI

Tutti i fior?

Only I knew it . . .
only I, who love him.

Can you see how foolish your doubts
were?
He has come! He has come! He has
come!
Just at the very moment
when everyone was saying:
weep and despair,
my love triumphs!
My love and my faith
triumph completely.
He has returned and he loves me!

Shake a branch
of that cherry-tree and cover me
with blossom.
I want to plunge
my burning brow
into its fragrant shower.

SUZUKI

Madam,
calm yourself . . . such weeping . . .

BUTTERFLY

No, I'm laughing, I'm laughing! How
long
shall we have to wait for him?
What do you think? An hour?

SUZUKI

Longer than that.

BUTTERFLY

Two hours, perhaps.
Everywhere must be as full of flowers,
as the night is of stars.

Go and gather the flowers!

SUZUKI

All the flowers?

BUTTERFLY

Tutti i fior, tutti, tutti.
Pesco, viola, gelsomin,
quanto di cespo, o d'erba,
o d'albero fiorì.

SUZUKI

Uno squallor d'inverno
sarà tutto il giardin.

BUTTERFLY

Tutta la primavera
voglio che olezzi qui.

SUZUKI

Uno squallor d'inverno
sarà tutto il giardin.
A voi, signora.

BUTTERFLY

Cogline ancora.

SUZUKI

Soventi a questa siepe
veniste a riguardare
lungi, piangendo
nella deserta immensità.

BUTTERFLY

Giunse l'atteso,
nulla più chiedo al mare;
diedi il pianto alla zolla,
essa i suoi fior mi dà!

SUZUKI

Spoglio è l'orto.

BUTTERFLY

Spoglio è l'orto? Vien, m'aiuta.

BUTTERFLY

All the flowers, all, all.
Peach blossom, violets, jasmine—
every bush, plant
and tree that's in bloom.

SUZUKI

The whole garden will be
like the dreary winter.

BUTTERFLY

I want all the fragrance
of spring in here.

SUZUKI

The whole garden will be
like the dreary winter.
There, madam.

BUTTERFLY

Pick some more.

SUZUKI

You used to come so often
to this hedge to gaze
for a long time, in tears,
over the empty sea.

BUTTERFLY

The long-awaited one has come,
I ask nothing more of the sea;
I have given my tears to the soil,
and it gives its flowers to me!

SUZUKI

The garden is bare.

BUTTERFLY

The garden is bare? Then come and
help me.

SUZUKI

Rose al varco della soglia.

BUTTERFLY, SUZUKI

Tutta la primavera voglio che olezzi
qui.
Seminiamo intorno april, seminiamo
april.
Tutta la primavera, *etc.*

SUZUKI

Gigli? viole?

BUTTERFLY

Intorno, intorno spandi.

SUZUKI

Seminiamo, *etc.*

BUTTERFLY

Seminiamo, *etc.*
Il suo sedil . . .

. . . s'inghirlandi, di convolvi
s'inghirlandi!

SUZUKI

Gigli, rose spandi; tutta la primavera!

BUTTERFLY

Gigli e viole intorno spandi!

SUZUKI

Spandi gigli, viole!

BUTTERFLY, SUZUKI

Seminiamo intorno april!
Gettiamo a mani piene
mammole e tuberose,
corolle di verbene,
petali d'ogni fior!

SUZUKI

Roses around the entrance.

BUTTERFLY, SUZUKI

I want all the fragrance of spring in
here.
Let us sow April all around.
I want all the fragrance, *etc.*

SUZUKI

Lilies? Violets?

BUTTERFLY

Everywhere, scatter them around.

SUZUKI

Let us sow, *etc.*

BUTTERFLY

Let us sow, *etc.*
His chair . . .

. . . let us garland with flowers!

SUZUKI

Lilies, roses, scatter around; the whole
of spring!

BUTTERFLY

Scatter lilies and violets all around!

SUZUKI

Scatter lilies and violets!

BUTTERFLY, SUZUKI

Let us sow April all around!
Let us scatter handfuls
of violets and tuberoses,
blossoms of verbena,
petals of every flower!

BUTTERFLY

Or vienmi ad adornar.
No! Pria portami il bimbo.
Non son più quella!
Troppi sospiri la bocca mandò,
e l'occhio riguardò
nel lontan troppo fiso.

Dammi sul viso
un tocco di carminio . . .
ed anche a te, piccino,
perchè la veglia non ti faccia vote
pel pallore le gote.

SUZUKI

Non vi movete
che v'ho a ravviare i capelli.

BUTTERFLY

Che ne diranno!
E lo zio Bonzo?
Già del mio danno
tutti contenti!
E Yamadori
coi suoi languori!
Beffati, scornati,
beffati, spennati,
gli ingrati!

SUZUKI

È fatto.

BUTTERFLY

L'obi che vestii da sposa.
Qua ch'io lo vesta.
Vo' che mi veda indosso
il vel del primo dì.
E un papavero rosso
nei capelli . . . Così.
Nello *shoshi* or farem
tre forellini
per riguardar,
e starem
zitti come topolini
ad aspettar.

BUTTERFLY

Now, come and help me dress.
No! First bring me the child.
How I've changed!
Too many sighs have passed these lips,
and these eyes have gazed
into the distance for too long.

Give my cheeks
a touch of rouge . . .
and some for you, too, little one,
so that the vigil will not
leave your cheeks pale.

SUZUKI

Now keep still,
so that I can do your hair.

BUTTERFLY

What will they say now!
And my uncle, the Bonze?
All of them so glad
I was deserted.
And Yamadori
with his languishing sighs!
Ridiculed, disgraced,
mocked, shown up,
the wretches!

SUZUKI

I've finished.

BUTTERFLY

The sash I wore as a bride,
bring it for me to put on.
I want him to see me dressed
as I was on that first day.
And a red poppy
in my hair . . . like that.
Now in the paper wall we'll make
three little holes
to look through,
and we'll keep
as quiet as mice,
and wait.

(Butterfly conduce il bambino presso lo shosi, e fa tre forti nello shosi: uno alto per se, uno più basso per Suzuki ed il terzo ancor più basso pel bimbo. Suzuki si accoscia e spia all'esterno. Butterfly si pone innanzi al foro più alto e spiando da esso rimane immobile, rigida come una statua; il bimbo, che sta fra la madre e Suzuki, guarda fuori curiosamente. È notte; i raggi lunari illuminano dall'esterno lo shosi. Da lontano si sentono le voci che cantano a bocca chiusa.)

(Butterfly leads the child to the shosi, and makes three holes in it—a high one for herself, one lower down for Suzuki and the third lower still for the child. Suzuki crouches down and looks out. Butterfly stands in front of the highest hole and looking out, stays quite still, as motionless as a statue; the child, standing between his mother and Suzuki, looks out curiously. It is night: the rays of the moon light up the shosi from the outside. From the distance can be heard the sound of voices humming.)

ATTO SECONDO

ACT II

PARTE SECONDA

PART 2

(Butterfly, sempre immobile, spia al di fuori: il bimbo dorme e dorme pure Suzuki.)

(Butterfly, still motionless, looks out: the baby is asleep, and so is Suzuki.)

MARINAI

Oh eh! Oh eh! Oh eh! Oh eh!

SAILORS

Heave-ho! Heave-ho!

SUZUKI

Già il sole! Ciociosan.

SUZUKI

It's sunrise already! Cho-Cho-San.

BUTTERFLY

Verrà, verrà, vedrai.

BUTTERFLY

He will come, he will come, you'll see.

SUZUKI

Salite a riposare, affranta siete . . .
al suo venire vi chiamerò.

SUZUKI

You must rest, you're worn out . . .
I'll call you when he comes.

BUTTERFLY

Dormi, amor mio,
dormi sul mio cor.
Tu sei con Dio
ed io col mio dolor.
A te i rai
degli astri d'or,
bimbo mio, dormi!

BUTTERFLY

Sleep, my love,
sleep on my breast.
You are with God,
and I am with my sorrow.
On you may the rays
of the golden stars shine,
sleep, my child, sleep!

SUZUKI

Povera Butterfly!

BUTTERFLY

Dormi, amor mio, *etc.*

SUZUKI

Povera Butterfly!
Chi sia?
Oh!

SHARPLESS

Stz!

PINKERTON

Zitta! Zitta!

SHARPLESS

Zitta! Zitta!

PINKERTON

Non la destar.

SUZUKI

Era stanca sì tanto.

Vi stette ad aspettare
tutta la notte col bimbo.

PINKERTON

Come sapea?

SUZUKI

Non giunge da tre anni
una nave nel porto
che da lunge Butterfly
non ne scruti
il color, la bandiera.

SHARPLESS

Ve lo dissi?

SUZUKI

Poor Butterfly!

BUTTERFLY

Sleep, my love, *etc.*

SUZUKI

Poor Butterfly!
Who can that be?
Oh!

SHARPLESS

Sssh!

PINKERTON

Hush! Hush!

SHARPLESS

Hush! Hush!

PINKERTON

Don't wake her.

SUZUKI

She was so very tired!

She stood waiting for you
all night, with the child.

PINKERTON

How did she know?

SUZUKI

For the past three years,
not a ship has put into port
without Butterfly
examining from here
its colour and flag.

SHARPLESS

Didn't I tell you so?

SUZUKI

La chiamo.

PINKERTON

No, non ancor.

SUZUKI

Lo vedete, ier sera,
la stanza volle sparger di fiori.

SHARPLESS

Ve lo dissi?

PINKERTON

Che pena!

SUZUKI

Chi c'è la fuori
nel giardino? Una donna!

PINKERTON

Zitta!

SUZUKI

Chi è? chi è?

SHARPLESS

Meglio dirle ogni cosa.

SUZUKI

Chi è? chi è?

PINKERTON

E venuta con me.

SUZUKI

Chi è? chi è?

SHARPLESS

È sua moglie!

SUZUKI

I'll call her.

PINKERTON

No, not yet.

SUZUKI

Look, last night
she insisted on scattering flowers
everywhere.

SHARPLESS

Didn't I tell you?

PINKERTON

This is dreadful!

SUZUKI

Who is that out there
in the garden? A woman!

PINKERTON

Hush!

SUZUKI

Who is it? Who is it?

SHARPLESS

Better tell her everything.

SUZUKI

Who is it? Who is it?

PINKERTON

She came with me.

SUZUKI

Who is it? Who is it?

SHARPLESS

It's his wife!

SUZUKI

Anime sante degli avi! Alla piccina
s'è spento il sol!

SHARPLESS

Scegliemmo quest'ora mattutina
per ritrovarti sola, Suzuki,
e alla gran prova un aiuto,
un sostegno cercar con te.

SUZUKI

Che giova? che giova?

SHARPLESS

Io so che alle sue pene
non ci sono conforti!
Ma del bimbo conviene
assicurar le sorti!

PINKERTON

Oh! . . .
. . . l'amara fragranza . . .

SHARPLESS

La pietosa . . .

PINKERTON

. . . di questi fior, . . .

SHARPLESS

. . . che entrar non . . .
. . . osa materna cura . . .

PINKERTON

. . . velenosa al cor mi va.

SHARPLESS

. . . del bimbo avrà!

SUZUKI

Holy spirits of my ancestors! For the
little one the sun has set!

SHARPLESS

We chose this early hour
to find you alone, Suzuki,
and in this hour of trial
to ask for your help and support.

SUZUKI

What's the use? What's the use?

SHARPLESS

I know that for her grief
there is no comfort.
But the child's future
we must make secure!

PINKERTON

Oh! . . .
. . . the bitter perfume . . .

SHARPLESS

That kind woman . . .

PINKERTON

. . . of these flowers . . .

SHARPLESS

. . . who dares not . . .
. . . come in, will care like a mother . . .

PINKERTON

. . . is like poison to my heart.

SHARPLESS

. . . for the child!

SUZUKI

Oh me trista!

PINKERTON

Immutata è la stanza dei nostri amor.

SUZUKI

E volete ch'io chieda ad una madre . . .

SHARPLESS

Suvvia, parla, suvvia . . .
. . . parla con quella . . .

PINKERTON

Ma un gel di morte vi sta.

SHARPLESS

. . . pia e . . .

SUZUKI

. . . e volete ch'io chieda . . .
'. . . ad una madre . . .

SHARPLESS

. . . conducila qui.

PINKERTON

Il mio ritratto!

SUZUKI

. . . Oh! me trista!

SHARPLESS

S'anche la . . .
'. . . veda Butterfly, . . .
. . . non importa.

SUZUKI

Oh, me . . .
. . . trista!

SUZUKI

Oh, how unhappy I am!

PINKERTON

Unchanged is the room where we were
in love.

SUZUKI

And you want me to ask a mother, . . .

SHARPLESS

Come, speak, . . .
. . . speak to that . . .

PINKERTON

But the chill of death is here.

SHARPLESS

. . . kind lady and . . .

SUZUKI

. . . you want me to ask . . .
. . . a mother . . .

SHARPLESS

. . . bring her in here.

PINKERTON

My picture!

SUZUKI

. . . Oh, how unhappy I am!

SHARPLESS

Even if . . .
. . . Butterfly sees her, . . .
. . . it doesn't matter.

SUZUKI

Oh, how . . .
. . . unhappy I am!

PINKERTON

Tre anni . . .

SHARPLESS

Anzi, meglio se accorta . . .

PINKERTON

. . . son passati, . . .

SHARPLESS

. . . del vero si facesse alla . . .

PINKERTON

. . . tre anni son passati, . . .

SUZUKI

Anime sante degli avi! alla piccina s'è
spento . . .

SHARPLESS

. . . sua vista. Suvvia, . . .

PINKERTON

. . . tre anni son passati . . .

SUZUKI

. . . il sol! Oh! me trista!

SHARPLESS

. . . parla con quella pia, . . .

PINKERTON

. . . e noverati n'ha . . .

SUZUKI

Anime sante degli avi!

PINKERTON

. . . i giorni . . .

PINKERTON

Three years . . .

SHARPLESS

On the contrary, better for her . . .

PINKERTON

. . . have passed, . . .

SHARPLESS

. . . to realise the truth through . . .

PINKERTON

. . . three years have passed, . . .

SUZUKI

Holy spirits of my ancestors! For the
little one the sun . . .

SHARPLESS

. . . seeing her. Come, . . .

PINKERTON

. . . three years have passed . . .

SUZUKI

. . . has set! Oh, how unhappy I am!

SHARPLESS

. . . speak to that kind lady, . . .

PINKERTON

. . . and she has been counting . . .

SUZUKI

Holy spirits of my ancestors!

PINKERTON

. . . the days . . .

146

SHARPLESS

. . . suvvia, conducila qui, conducila
qui!

PINKERTON

. . . e l'ore, i giorni e l'ore!

SUZUKI

Alla piccina s'è spento il sol!

SHARPLESS

Vien, Suzuki, vien!

PINKERTON

Non posso rimaner, . . .

SUZUKI

Oh! me trista!

PINKERTON

. . . Sharpless, v'aspetto per via.

SHARPLESS

Non ve l'avevo detto?

PINKERTON

Datele voi qualche soccorso.
Mi struggo dal rimorso.

SHARPLESS

Vel dissi? Vi ricorda?
Quando la man vi diede:
'Badate! Ella ci crede'—
e fui profeta allor!
Sorda al consigli, sorda
ai dubbi, vilipesa,
nell'ostinata attesa
raccolse il cor.

SHARPLESS

. . . and bring her in here!

PINKERTON

. . . and even the hours!

SUZUKI

For the little one the sun has set!

SHARPLESS

Come, Suzuki, come!

PINKERTON

I can't stay here, . . .

SUZUKI

Oh, how unhappy I am!

PINKERTON

. . . Sharpless, I'll wait for you on the
way down.

SHARPLESS

Did I not tell you?

PINKERTON

You must give her some comfort.
I am overcome with remorse.

SHARPLESS

I told you, didn't I? Do you remember?
When she gave you her hand,
'Take care,' I said, 'she trusts you'—
and I spoke prophetically!
Deaf to advice, deaf
to doubt, vilified,
she has waited obstinately
and with devotion.

PINKERTON

Sì, tutto in un istante
io vedo il fallo mio,
e sento che di questo tormento
tregua mai non avrò! No!

SHARPLESS

Andate: il triste vero
da sola apprenderà.

PINKERTON

Addio, fiorito asil
di letizia e d'amor.
Sempre il mite suo sembiante
con strazio atroce vedrò.

SHARPLESS

Ma or quel cor sincero
presago è già.

PINKERTON

Addio, fiorito asil . . .

SHARPLESS

Vel dissi . . . vi ricorda?
E fui profeta allor.

PINKERTON

. . . Non reggo al tuo squallor, ah, non
reggo, *etc.*
Fuggo, fuggo, ah, son vil!
Addio, non reggo al tuo . . .
. . . squallor, ah! son vil, . . .

SHARPLESS

Andate, il triste vero apprenderà.

PINKERTON

. . . ah! son vil!

PINKERTON

Yes, all at once
I see my mistake,
and I feel I shall never find
respite from this torment. No!

SHARPLESS

Go: she shall learn
the sad truth alone.

PINKERTON

Farewell, flowery refuge
of happiness and love.
Her gentle face will always haunt me,
torturing me forever.

SHARPLESS

But now that faithful heart
already has a premonition.

PINKERTON

Farewell, flowery refuge . . .

SHARPLESS

I told you, didn't I? Do you remember?
And I spoke prophetically.

PINKERTON

. . . I cannot bear your sad appearance,
oh, I cannot bear, *etc.*
I must fly, I am contemptible!
Farewell, I cannot bear your . . .
. . . sad appearance, ah! I am
contemptible . . .

SHARPLESS

Go, she shall learn the sad truth.

PINKERTON

. . . oh, I am contemptible!

KATE PINKERTON

Glielo dirai?

SUZUKI

Prometto.

KATE

E la darai consiglio
d'affidarmi?

SUZUKI

Prometto.

KATE

Lo terrò come un figlio.

SUZUKI

Vi credo. Ma bisogna
ch'io le sia sola accanto.
Nella grande ora sola!
Piangerà tanto, tanto,
piangerà tanto!

BUTTERFLY

Suzuki! Suzuki! Dove sei? Suzuki!

SUZUKI

Son qui . . . pregavo
e rimettevo a posto.

No! No! No! No! No!
Non scendete! No! No!

BUTTERFLY

È qui, è qui . . . dove è nascosto?

È qui, è qui!
Ecco il Console . . .
E dove, dove?
Non c'è!
Quella donna?
Che vuol da me?

KATE PINKERTON

Will you tell her?

SUZUKI

I promise.

KATE

And will you advise her
to trust me?

SUZUKI

I promise.

KATE

I shall care for him like my own son.

SUZUKI

I believe you. But I must
be alone with her.
At such a dreadful hour, alone!
She'll weep so much,
so much!

BUTTERFLY

Suzuki! Suzuki! Where are you?
Suzuki!

SUZUKI

I'm here . . . I was praying
and tidying up.

No! No!
Don't come in! No! No!

BUTTERFLY

He's here, he's here . . . where is he
hiding?
He's here, he's here!
There's the Consul . . .
Where? Where?
He isn't here!
Who is that woman?
What does she want of me?

Niuno parla!
Perchè piangete?

No. Non ditemi nulla . . . nulla . . .
forse potrei cader
morta sull'attimo.
Tu, Suzuki, che sei
tanto buona, non piangere!
E mi vuoi tanto bene,
un Sì, un No, dì piano . . .
Vive?

SUZUKI

Sì.

BUTTERFLY

Ma non viene più.
Te l'han detto!
Vespa! Voglio che tu risponda.

SUZUKI

Mai più.

BUTTERFLY

Ma è giunto ieri?

SUZUKI

Sì.

BUTTERFLY

Ah! quella donna
mi fa tanta paura!

SHARPLESS

È la causa innocente
d'ogni vostra sciagura.
Perdonatele.

BUTTERFLY

Ah! è sua moglie.
Tutto è morto per me!
Tutto è finito! Ah!

No-one speaks!
Why are you crying?

No. Don't tell me anything . . .
perhaps I might fall
dead on the spot.
You, Suzuki, who are
so kind, don't cry!
And if you love me,
tell me quietly 'Yes' or 'No' . . .
Is he alive?

SUZUKI

Yes.

BUTTERFLY

But he's not coming back.
They've told you!
Viper! You must answer me.

SUZUKI

He is not.

BUTTERFLY

But he arrived yesterday?

SUZUKI

Yes.

BUTTERFLY

Oh, that woman
makes me so afraid!

SHARPLESS

She is the innocent cause
of all your suffering.
Forgive her.

BUTTERFLY

Ah! She is his wife.
All is over for me!
All is finished! Ah!

SHARPLESS

Coraggio.

BUTTERFLY

Voglion prendermi tutto!
Il figlio mio!

SHARPLESS

Fatelo pel suo bene il sacrifizio.

BUTTERFLY

Ah! triste madre! Abbandonar mio
figlio!
E sia! A lui devo obbedir.

KATE

Potete perdonarmi, Butterfly?

BUTTERFLY

Sotto il gran ponte del cielo non v'è
donna di voi più felice.
Siatelo sempre,
non v'attristate per me.

KATE

Povera piccina!

SHARPLESS

È un'immensa pietà!

KATE

E il figlio lo darà?

BUTTERFLY

A lui lo potrò dare
se lo verrà a cercare.
Fra mezz'ora salite la collina.

SUZUKI

Come una mosca prigionera
l'ali batte il piccolo cuor!

SHARPLESS

Be brave.

BUTTERFLY

They want to take everything from me!
My son!

SHARPLESS

Make the sacrifice for his sake.

BUTTERFLY

Oh, unhappy mother! To give up my
son!
So be it! I must obey him.

KATE

Can you forgive me, Butterfly?

BUTTERFLY

Under the great arc of the sky, there is
no happier woman than you.
May you be happy always—
don't make yourself sad because of me.

KATE

Poor little thing!

SHARPLESS

What a terrible shame!

KATE

And will she give up the child?

BUTTERFLY

I shall give my child to him,
if he comes to fetch him himself.
In half an hour, come up the hill again.

SUZUKI

Like the wings of a captive fly
her little heart is beating!

151

BUTTERFLY

Troppo luce è di fuor,
e troppa primavera. Chiudi!

Il bimbo ove sia?

SUZUKI

Giuoca. Lo chiamo?

BUTTERFLY

Lascialo giuocar.
Va a fargli compagnia.

SUZUKI

Resto con voi.

BUTTERFLY

Va, va. Te lo comando.

'Con onor muore
chi non può serbar vita con onore.'

*S'apre la porta e vedesi il braccio di Suzuki
che spinge il bambino verso la madre.*

Tu? Tu? Tu? Tu?
Piccolo Iddio! Amore, amore mio,
fior di giglio e di rosa.
Non saperlo mai—
per te,
per tuoi puri occhi,
muor Butterfly,
perchè tu possa andar
di là dal mare
senza che ti rimorda,
ai dì maturi,
il materno abbandono.
O a me, sceso dal trono
dell'alto Paradiso,
guarda ben fiso, fiso
di tua madre la faccia,
che ten resti una traccia,
guarda ben!

BUTTERFLY

There's too much light from outside,
and it's too much like spring. Close the
shutters!

Where is the baby?

SUZUKI

He's playing. Shall I call him?

BUTTERFLY

Let him play.
Go and keep him company.

SUZUKI

I shall stay with you.

BUTTERFLY

Go, go. I command you.

'He dies with honour
who can no longer live with honour.'

*The door opens and the arm of Suzuki appears,
pushing the child towards his mother.*

You? You? You?
Little idol! My love, flower of the lily
and the rose.
May you never know that,
for your sake,
for the sake of your innocent eyes,
Butterfly died,
so that you may go
far away across the sea
and never feel pain
in later days,
at your mother's desertion.
Oh, my own, descended from the
throne
of high Paradise,
look carefully on your
mother's face,
so that you may keep a memory
of it, look carefully!

Amore, addio!
Addio, piccolo amor!
Va. Gioca, gioca.

*(Prende il bambino, lo posa su di una stuoia,
gli dà nelle mani la banderuola americana e
una pupattola e lo invita a trastullarsene,
mentre delicatemente gli benda gli occhi. Poi
afferra il coltello e va dietro il paravento. Si
vede Butterfly sporgersi fuori dal paravento, e
brancolando muovere verso il bambino. Il gran
velo bianco le circonda il collo, si trascina
verso il bambino, poi gli cade vicino.)*

PINKERTON

(interno)

Butterfly! Butterfly! Butterfly!

*(Pinkerton e Sharpless si precipitano nella
stanza, accorrendo presso Butterfly che con
debole gesto indica il bambino e muore.
Pinkerton si inginocchia, mentre Sharpless
prende il bambino.)*

Farewell, my love!
My little love, farewell!
Go. Play, play.

*(She takes the child, sits him on a mat, puts
into his hands the American flag and a doll,
and persuades him to play with them, while
she gently blindfolds him. Then she takes the
sword and goes behind the screen. Butterfly
reaches out from behind the screen, and
staggers towards the child. With the white
veil round her neck, she drags herself towards
the child, then collapses near him.)*

PINKERTON

(from outside)

Butterfly! Butterfly! Butterfly!

*(Pinkerton and Sharpless rush into the room,
and run towards Butterfly, who with a feeble
gesture points to the child and dies. Pinkerton
kneels, while Sharpless takes the child.)*

CURTAIN

Chronology

Major Compositions

Further Reading

Chronology

1858   Puccini born on 22 December, at Lucca in Tuscany. He represented the fifth generation of a family of church composers who had occupied the post of organist and choirmaster at Lucca's Cathedral of San Martino from about the first third of the eighteenth century. The post was handed down from father to son: Giacomo (1712–81)—Antonio (1747–1832)—Domenico (1771–1815)—Michele (1813–64). At the age of ten, Puccini became a choir boy at San Martino and San Michele, and studied at the Lucca Conservatoire (then Conservatorio Pacini, now Conservatorio Luigi Boccherini), passing his exams in 1880 with a Mass in four parts. A visit to Pisa four years earlier (March 1876) to see Verdi's *Aida* decided Puccini to follow an operatic career.

1880   Further studies at the Milan Conservatorio Reale (now Conservatorio Giuseppe Verdi) under Antonio Bazzini and Amilcare Ponchielli, best known as the composer of *La Gioconda* (1876).

1883   Received diploma as 'Maestro' in June, with the school-leaving exercise *Capriccio Sinfonico*, performed with great success by the student orchestra on 13 July under the famous Franco Faccio, a conductor much esteemed by Verdi.

1884   In April of the previous year, Puccini had decided to take part in the *Concorso Sonzogno*, the first of several prize competitions promoted by the publisher Edoardo Sonzogno for the best one-act opera. (In 1890 Mascagni's *Cavalleria rusticana* was discovered in this way.) Puccini sent in *Le Villi*, which was not even mentioned by the jury when it announced the result of the competition. Through the help of influential Milan personalities (Boito, Ponchielli, Marco De Sala), the opera was staged at the Teatro dal Verme, Milan, on 31 May, and achieved great acclaim. The publisher Giulio Ricordi acquired *Le Villi*, making Puccini extend it into a two-act work (Turin, 26 December), and commissioned from him another opera, *Edgar*. Puccini, aged 26, eloped with Elvira Bonturi-Gemignani, the wife of a Lucca merchant, who took her daughter, Fosca, with her. Tonio, their only son, was born in 1886.

1889 *Edgar* performed at La Scala, Milan, on 21 April, with the famous Romilda Pantaleoni (Verdi's first Desdemona) and Aurelia Cataneo (the first Italian Isolde) in the leading female roles. A near-fiasco. At Ricordi's suggestion, Puccini reduced the four acts to three, in the process maiming the work. Revised in 1892 and 1905.

1891 Puccini settled at Torre del Lago by the lake of Massaciuccoli, which he had first visited in 1884. Then a primitive fishing village, the place gave the composer the seclusion he needed for his work, and allowed him to indulge his passion for shooting wildfowl, for which the lake was famous. Puccini was to live at Torre for the next thirty years.

1893 *Manon Lescaut* was the first of Puccini's operas for which the composer, prompted by the success of Massenet's *Manon* (1884), chose the subject himself. It was given at Turin on 1 February, with a success never achieved by any of his subsequent works, and made his name known internationally. At least four pairs of hands worked on the libretto—Leoncavallo, the writer Marco Praga, the poet Domenico Oliva and Luigi Illica. That is why *Manon Lescaut* was published without the names of the librettists—a unique case in the history of nineteenth-century opera.

1896 *La Bohème* was first produced at Turin on 1 February. There was much hostility shown towards the work by a large majority of the critics, and it was not until the performance at Palermo the following April that the opera conquered all Italy and subsequently the whole world. It was the first of his three most popular stage works in which the composer had the collaboration of Guiseppe Giacosa and Illica, who complemented each other perfectly and who were the best librettists he ever had.

1900 The *première* of *Tosca*, the action of which is set in Rome, was, given, appropriately, in the Italian capital, at the Teatro Costanzi on 14 January. It was Puccini's first step into *verismo* (the Italian for 'realism').

1904 In January, in a religious ceremony, Puccini married Elvira, whose husband had died the previous year. *Madam Butterfly*, first given at La Scala on 17 February, was one of the most resounding fiascos in operatic history. There is evidence that this was engineered by Puccini's rivals, who had also tried to wreck the *première* of *Tosca*. The revised version of the opera, given at Brescia on 28 May, was received with enthusiasm.

1905   Beginning of Puccini's friendship with Sybil Seligman, the wife of a London banker, who became his confidante in professional and, notably, private matters.

1909   In January, Doria Manfredi, a servant girl in the Puccinis' household, committed suicide because of accusations by Elvira that she entertained an intimate relationship with Puccini. A court case was brought against Elvira by Doria's parents, and the verdict went against her. The wide publicity that the so-called 'Doria Affair' received deeply affected the sensitive and highly vulnerable composer.

1910   *La Fanciulla del West* had its *première* at the Metropolitan Opera, New York. A star cast, with Emmy Destinn in the title role, Enrico Caruso as Johnson and Pasquale Amato as Sheriff Rance, was conducted by Toscanini.

1915   After the outbreak of World War I Puccini was accused of pro-German sentiments, which caused a serious rift between him and Toscanini.

1917   *La Rondine*, a hybrid between operetta and opera, was first staged at Monte Carlo, on 27 March. This 'Austrian' work, so-called by Puccini because it originated in a suggestion by the two directors of Vienna's Carl Theater, involved him in a sensational political scandal with the chauvinist circles round the Paris paper, *L'Action française.*

1918   First production of *Il Trittico* at the Metropolitan Opera on 14 December. It consists of three one-act operas—*Il Tabarro* (realistic melodrama), *Suor Angelica* (sentimental tragedy) and *Gianni Schicchi* (Florentine comedy). Subsequently, and much against Puccini's wishes, *Gianni Schicchi*, the most successful of the three operas, was performed by itself; latterly, *Il Tabarro* has come into its own, and there are now occasional productions of the whole Triptych.

1921   In December, Puccini left his beloved Torre del Lago on account of disturbing industrial developments, and moved to his villa at Viareggio, where he had bought land in 1915.

1923   On 1 February, Toscanini, who had made his peace with Puccini, conducted a revival of *Manon Lescaut* at La Scala, in commemoration of the thirtieth anniversary of the opera's *première.*

1924   Puccini was nominated 'Senator of the Realm' by Mussolini. In the autumn, a persistent throat complaint was diagnosed as an advanced cancer. In early November Puccini entered a Brussels clinic in order to undergo X-ray treatment, but his heart failed and he died in the early hours of 29 November, aged nearly 66.

1926 *Turandot,* on which Puccini had been working since 1920, was produced at La Scala on 25 April. At this performance the opera ended where Puccini had left off before his journey to Brussels (Death of Liù). The next evening it was played with the last two scenes completed by Franco Alfano from Puccini's sketches.

Major Compositions

(The dates in brackets are those of first performances.)

Mass for Four Voices and Orchestra (Lucca, 1880)

Capriccio Sinfonico (Milan, 1883)

Le Villi (Milan, 1884)

Edgar (Milan, 1889; rev. versions, Ferrara, 1892, and Buenos Aires, 1905)

Manon Lescaut (Turin, 1893)

La Bohème (Turin, 1896)

Madama Butterfly (Milan, February 1904; rev. version, Brescia, May 1904)

La Fanciulla del West (New York, 1910)

La Rondine (Monte Carlo, 1917)

Il Trittico: Il Tabarro, Suor Angelica, Gianni Schicchi (New York, 1918)

Turandot (Milan, 1926)

Further Reading

Adami, G. and Carner, M. (ed): *The Letters of Giacomo Puccini* (London, 1974)
Ashbrook, William: *The Operas of G. Puccini* (London, 1969)
Carner, Mosco: *Puccini. A Critical Biography* (London, 1958; enlrgd. edition, 1974)
Greenfield, Edward: *Puccini. The Keeper of the Seal* (London, 1958)
Hughes, Spike: *Famous Puccini Operas* (London, 1959)
Newman, Ernest: *More Opera Nights* (London, 1954)
Seligman, Vincent: *Puccini Among Friends* (London, 1938)

Acknowledgments

The illustrations are reproduced by kind permission of the following: Alec Murray: 38, 79; Clive Barda: 37, 42; Covent Garden Archives (Angelo Hornak): 55, 56, 63, 69; Donald Southern: 33, 35; EMI Records (Angus McBean): 6; Houston Rogers: 65; Keystone Press Agency: 49, 52, 83; Lyric Opera of Chicago (Nancy Sorenson): 81, 82; Mansell Collection: 72; Metropolitan Opera Archives: 48 (Louis Mélançon), 75; Mosco Carner (Author's collection): 18; Museo di Torre del Lago Puccini (from *Puccini nelle Immagini*, Garzanti 1949): 13, 16, 17, 28, 46; New Orleans Opera House (Thoma Kersh): 51; New York City Opera (Fred Fehl): 84; Opera Magazine: 14, 20, 33, 38, 40, 49, 51, 61, 66, 78, 79, 80, 81, 82, 84; Radio Times Hulton Picture Library: 11, 25, 47, 78; Raymond Mander and Joe Mitchenson Theatre Collection: 27, 70; Städt Theatre Leipzig: 49; Teatro alla Scala (Erio Piccagliani): 34, 77; Teatro Comunale, Florence (Foto Marchiori): 66; Trustees of the British Museum: 23; Welsh National Opera (Julian Sheppard): 40; Zoe Dominic: 80.